Selections from

HISTORY TODAY

General Editor
C. M. D. CROWDER

AMERICAN PROFILES

A Selection of Articles from *History Today*
with an original introductory essay by

ESMOND WRIGHT

OLIVER & BOYD

EDINBURGH

LONDON

OLIVER AND BOYD LTD

Tweeddale Court
Edinburgh 1

39A Welbeck Street
London W 1

First published 1967

1 03151

© 1967 Esmond Wright

Printed in Great Britain by
T. and A. Constable Ltd.
Edinburgh

PREFACE

If it was courageous to try to identify the major themes in
the American story in the companion volume to this, it is
positively foolhardy to try to identify in a few paragraphs
the characteristics of the American people or of their
leaders. For they have come from all over the globe and
their story is, in one of its aspects, simply a commentary
on one of the greatest folk-wanderings in history.

> The homesick men begot high-cheekboned things
> Whose wit was whittled with a different sound
> And Thames and all the rivers of the kings
> Ran into Mississippi and were drowned.
>
> They planted England with a stubborn trust.
> But the cleft dust was never English dust.
>
> Stepchild of every exile from content
> And all the disavouched, hard-bitten pack
> Shipped overseas to steal a continent
> With neither shirts nor honor to their back.
>
> Pimping grandee and rump-faced regicide,
> Apple-cheeked younkers from a windmill-square,
> Puritans stubborn as the nails of Pride,
> Rakes from Versailles and thieves from County Clare,
>
> The black-robed priests who broke their hearts in vain
> To make you God and France or God and Spain.[1]

[1] Stephen Vincent Benet, *John Brown's Body*. London (Heinemann)
1945, p. 2.

Nor is it necessary to seek for common features in the careers or personalities of the six men whose activities are assessed here. All that need be said is that each of them was important, each was sharply individualistic, and each was highly complex. Their biographies need no gloss added to their own intrinsic fascination.

Acknowledgements are due to the estate of the late Stephen Vincent Benet for permission to quote from *John Brown's Body* (copyright 1927, 1928 by Stephen Vincent Benet, copyright renewed 1955, 1956 by Rosemary Carr Benet); and from "Western Wagons", *A Book of Americans* (copyright 1933 by Rosemary and Stephen Vincent Benet, copyright renewed 1961 by Rosemary Carr Benet).

ESMOND WRIGHT

CONTENTS

OF PRESIDENTS
AND FOUNDING FATHERS

Of the six men whose stories are told here, four were Presidents. Franklin was the most revered figure at the Constitutional Convention in 1787, and the one who came nearest, be it said, to revealing the secrets of Independence Hall. Hamilton, who steered the engine of Washington's statecraft, and was both his pen-man and his first lieutenant in war and peace, was the major architect of the Constitution; he merited and sought the Presidency but was denied it by his foreign birth, by his frankly pro-British and aristocratic political leanings, and by his arrogance. What can safely be said of all six is that they made decisive contributions to American history, that without them history at key points would have taken an entirely different direction, and that the creation and development of the office of the Presidency was their major achievement.

Washington permanently set his own personal stamp on the office, which in some measure was built with him in mind as its first occupant. Hamilton saw executive power as fundamental to the survival and growth of the new state; and American economic history a century later was not much more than an elaboration of his policies. Lincoln, Wilson, and F. D. Roosevelt steadily increased its authority and made it, as it is today, the single most important elective office in the world. So that

perhaps the first theme to emphasise as central to the
activity of these men is the nature of the office that they
either held or helped to create, the Presidency. Its power
today is their primary achievement.

That power takes a number of forms. First, the President is the head of the Executive. He is responsible today
for the loyalty, the efficiency, and the conduct of over
two million Americans in the Federal administration; he
appoints to all major diplomatic posts and to Supreme
Court judgeships, given that two-thirds of the Senators
agree; in recent years a succession of Re-organisation
Acts have even strengthened his leadership; and he has
the final and awesome task, as the Constitution puts it, to
"take care that the laws be faithfully executed"—even if
this means that he has to employ troops or to Federalise
the National Guard to do so, as President Kennedy had
to do in 1962 in Alabama. Harry Truman characteristically described his job by the notice on his desk—"The
buck stops here".

Second, he is responsible for the country's foreign
policy. Technically he shares authority here with Congress, and especially with the Senate which must approve
by a two-thirds vote not only his appointments but all
treaties, and all declarations of peace and war. Some
Presidents delegate foreign policy to the Secretary of
State, as did Eisenhower to Dulles. Some make him
almost a nonentity as F. D. Roosevelt made Cordell
Hull.

Third, he is Commander-in-Chief of the armed forces
and certainly in all crises the President's powers are
virtually those of a dictator. The need in wartime for

secrecy and speed give him near-autocratic powers; he decides where troops shall be stationed, and often in doing so decides whom they shall fight—even if acts of war are declared not by him but by Congress. By using his power to make executive agreements, he can by-pass Congressional control; of seventy-five agreements with foreign governments made in 1944 by President Roosevelt, only one went through Congress. And these wartime powers have cut sharply into the domestic lives of Americans. In World War II, F. D. Roosevelt created a host of emergency boards; he seized and operated more than sixty strike-bound or strike-threatened industries; he evacuated seventy thousand American citizens of Japanese descent from the West coast; all as part of his function as Commander-in-Chief. In October 1962 in the Cuban crisis President Kennedy alerted the armed forces and had American ships ready to blockade Castro's Cuba.

Fourth, the President is the nation's chief legislator. The Constitution empowers the President "to give to the Congress Information of the State of the Union and recommend to their Consideration such Measures as he shall judge necessary and expedient": witness the tax cuts, the civil rights legislation, the foreign aid programme that President Johnson pushed through Congress in the first year of his Presidency. The President has in fact great initiative in legislation. Of course, his office is distinct from Congress. He does not sit *in* Congress, nor do his Cabinet officers; there is no responsibility *to* Congress. Yet in some measure ever since Woodrow Wilson's day the President has been in effect a sort of

prime minister, cajoling, persuading, exhorting, demanding. Indeed, when a President—like Eisenhower—
has failed to act as Congressional leader from without,
the machine has lost its momentum.

Fifth, the President is Chief not only of government but of state, the supreme ceremonial figure of the
nation.

Sixth, he is an *elective* monarch. He is also head of
his party, an all-the-year-round political boss. He is
distributor of patronage, main prop of fellow-candidates,
one who should be—and like F. D. Roosevelt often was
—on first-name terms with every other political boss in
each of the three thousand counties in the United States,
a miraculous back-slapper and speech-maker, not only
cajoler but calculator-in-chief.

And not least he is the leader of the nation and now, in
some measure, spokesman of the free world.

It is a formidable office, almost beyond the capacity,
one might think, of any man to fill, certainly beyond any
man's capacity to devise. For it was never planned in this
way. What the Founding Fathers, and certainly Franklin,
had in mind in 1787 was a wise, gentlemanly aristocrat
who would act as an arbiter in debate, more, indeed, a
magistrate than a leader. He was to be aloof from politics.
If there were a role for him to play it should be that of an
elective and temporary king, reigning but not ruling.
This prescription offered no problems to the Founders
since, from the outset, it was sober, cautious, undangerous
but physically impressive George Washington whom
they had in mind. The Founders did not even expect that
the President would campaign for his own election;

instead they devised what now seems in retrospect a most complicated bit of electoral mechanics, a system of indirect election by a college of non-partisan electors chosen locally through a then very restricted suffrage. The indirect election was designed to remove the President from direct popular control and to preserve the rights of the states from being swamped by centralised government. Madison thought that forty-nine times out of fifty the electors from each state would vote for a "favorite son" and thus throw the choice of the President to the House of Representatives where each state had a single vote. In fact this happened only twice, in 1800 and 1824. The growth of the party system transformed the vote of the Electoral College into a rubber stamp.

In 1824, although Andrew Jackson received more popular and electoral votes than did John Quincy Adams, the election fell into the House of Representatives, which elected Adams. In 1888, although Benjamin Harrison had nearly one hundred thousand fewer popular votes than Grover Cleveland, Harrison received 233 electoral votes to Cleveland's 168, and was elected President. In 1960, although Mr Kennedy scored a clear victory over Mr Nixon in the Electoral College, his popular majority was only 118,000 out of nearly sixty-nine million.

The development of an industrial society with its system of rapid transport and communications, especially radio and television, the broadening of the franchise, and the extension of public education have all made the processes of selecting and electing the President public and popular. And the same forces have gradually transformed the office itself. From the beginning authority and decision were thrust upon it. Even Washington when he approached the Senate and asked for advice on an Indian treaty was rebuffed by it; he had to make his own decisions and *then* persuade the Senate to ratify them. A number of Presidents have held to the view that they are but supreme magistrates—a "purely administrative officer" as President Ulysses Grant called himself. And, of course, after all wars there have been attempts by Congress to minimise the role of the President. It happened after Lincoln's assassination and, again, the 80th Congress in Harry Truman's Presidency sought to assert itself and to back-pedal on the President's initiative in foreign policy.

For by no means all the Presidents have been strong men. Indeed, perhaps only Jefferson, Jackson, Theodore Roosevelt, and Truman would merit being added to those described here as being truly great Presidents. Some have been machine politicians elevated into office like Warren Harding; some have been compromise choices (as was, in a measure, Lincoln, who reached the Presidency by devious roads); some have been heirs apparent who could not be avoided but were unwelcome nonetheless (John Adams); some have been cautious and hesitant men, Presidents by abnegation. Perhaps the best example of the President by abnegation is President Buchanan who in the great crisis of 1860 argued that he had no power to use force against the seceding Southern States. General Eisenhower, despite the sharp image of the D-Day Commander, always saw himself as a mediator; throughout the 1952 elections he talked of the need to end "Executive usurpations of power" and to

Calvinism as much as the log cabin is at the source of
the urge to political eminence in the New World.

Many leaders were, of course, born in log cabins, but it
should be remembered that on some frontiers these were
luxuries indeed, for this was in its origins, and away
from the colonial coast, a very poor New World. The log
cabin was a deliberately-cultivated myth as early as
William Harrison's election campaign in 1840; Old Tip
had much else to his credit besides a homespun coat[1]—
the frontier bred natural aristocrats as well as natural
democrats. And if Lincoln was very humbly born, Mary
Todd had a sharp, snobbish eye for a husband, as well as
a temper to try a saint.

If the concept of lowly origins as a guarantee of one's
democratic *bona fides* was soon well-established, the
tradition of public service did not originate in the log
cabin. The earliest tradition of all in the New World was
inherited from the Old; the sense common to New
England's town meetings and to the parishes of Tidewater
Virginia that in service to the local community the
citizen was fulfilling not only his social obligation but was
most fully being himself. The first tradition of all in
America was simply that of *noblesse oblige*, even if it was
an obligation imposed in the forest clearings. Its roots
were English and aristocratic. They were as strong in
Washington—whose half-brother had been educated
in England—as in Wilson or F. D. Roosevelt.

Yet it would be an impossible claim to see in these half-
dozen men American "types". If all had in them the

---

[1] "Benjamin Franklin", p. 43; "Lincoln Before his Election", p. 64.

qualities of the entrepreneur and the frontiersman—not least the first President—these qualities were tightly curbed and disciplined. Both about Washington and Lincoln their contemporaries always had a sense that the fires were controlled with difficulty, that the shoulders would strain and tear the uniform. And were this volume to be really representative, it ought to include the true frontiersmen, Davy Crockett or Jim Bridger or George Rogers Clark. Their story, however, has been amply chronicled, not least by F. J. Turner, the first great historian of the frontier in his famous paper delivered in 1893, *The Significance of the Frontier in American History*.

The Atlantic frontier was compounded of fisherman, fur-trader, miner, cattle-raiser, and farmer. Excepting the fisherman, each type of industry was on the march toward the West, impelled by an irresistible attraction. Each passed in successive waves across the continent. Stand at Cumberland Gap and watch the procession of civilization, marching single file—the buffalo following the trail to the salt springs, the Indian, the fur-trader and hunter, the cattle-raiser, the pioneer farmer—and the frontier has passed by. Stand at South Pass in the Rockies a century later and see the same procession with wider intervals between. The unequal rate of advance compels us to distinguish the frontier into the trader's frontier, the rancher's frontier, or the miner's frontier, and the farmer's frontier. When the mines and the cowpens were still near the fall line the trader's pack trains were tinkling across the Alleghenies, and the French on the Great Lakes were fortifying their posts, alarmed by the British trader's birch canoe. When the trappers scaled the Rockies, the farmers were still near the mouth of the Missouri.[2]

Such a land, said Turner, attracted all types, the gifted, the ruthless, the enterprising, the ne'er-do-well, the perennial misfits and the vagabonds. To Turner it was this moving belt of human population pushing ever-westwards that was the unique feature in the American story, and to it were due, he believed, many of the characteristics of American society: it was a safety-valve for urban tensions and discontents; it bred resourceful men and independence of mind; it was open to talent and unlimited in its possibilities, for free land was available to every man who had the energy, courage, and will to work it; it called for initiative and ingenuity and self-reliance; it was hostile to authority, it was activist, and it was strongly optimistic.

> They went with axe and rifle, when the trail was still
>   to blaze,
> They went with wife and children, in the prairie-
>   schooner days,
> With banjo and with frying pan—Susanna, don't you
>   cry!
> For I'm off to California to get rich out there or die!
> We've broken land and cleared it, but we're tired of
>   where we are.
> They say that wild Nebraska is a better place by far.
> There's gold in far Wyoming, there's black earth in
>   Ioway,
> So pack up the kids and blankets, for we're moving
>   out today!

[2] F. J. Turner, "The Significance of the Frontier in American History", in D. Boorstin, *An American Primer*. Chicago (University Press) 1966, p. 530.

The cowards never started and the weak died on the
  road,
And all across the continent the endless campfires
  glowed.
We'd taken land and settled—but a traveler passed by—
And we're going West tomorrow—Lordy, never ask
  us why!

We're going West tomorrow, where the promises
  can't fail.
O'er the hills in legions, boys, and crowd the dusty
  trail!
We shall starve and freeze and suffer. We shall die,
  and tame the lands.
But we're going West tomorrow, with our fortune in
  our hands.[3]

It had indeed no obvious limits: "Why, sir, on the north
we are bounded by the Aurora Borealis, on the east . . .
by the rising sun, on the south . . . by the procession of
the Equinoxes, and on the west by the Day of Judge-
ment." It was the uniqueness of this environment in
agriculture and topography which explained, Turner
believed, the differences between the Old World and the
New.

In recent years Turner's view has been contested. The
Tennessee and Kentucky frontier, it has been argued,
was marked less by dignity and democracy than by cheap
politics, crude individualism, and bigoted sectarianism.
Born of two parents, protestant fundamentalism and
radical democracy, its egalitarianism easily lapsed into
anti-intellectualism. The romantic exaltation of "the

[3] Stephen Vincent Benet, "Western Wagons", *The Stephen Vincent
Benet Pocket Book*. New York (Pocket Books) 1946, pp. 411-12.

common man", the celebration of "common sense" and "plain talk", the insistence that government is an activity which requires no special training or abilities, the distrust of speculation, the suspicion of intellectual authority, the equation of art with artifice—all this is in the mainstream of American democratic thought, which flows with little interruption (though many detours) from Tom Paine through Andrew Jackson to Joe McCarthy. The frontier has bred demagogues as well as democrats, Bryans as well as Lincolns. But this, too, is a world that has passed. The frontier was closed eighty years ago.

Contemporary America is the heir of that frontier story: it is polyglot in its people, continental in its scale, mobile and restless yet curiously conformist in its character. It has moved a long way from the simple and rural values of the eighteenth century, from the world of the open range, or even from the difficult moral, yet politically clear-cut, issues that faced Lincoln.

The portraits here are those of men of high individuality, who were not given to that easy orthodoxy of manners, of society or of creed that comes so readily today. And these essays are but profiles, outlines roughly etched like those on a Mount Rushmore that stands high above the plain folk on the plains. Success in today's America may call for other qualities, the qualities implied by David Riesman in his *The Lonely Crowd*. The magic word now is consensus; "come let us reason together", says the present incumbent of the White House, even if it is only his own formula for getting his own idiosyncratic way. In the career of as charismatic a leader as Kennedy, however, it is clear that behind the leading profile were many other profiles in the shadows, of brain trusters and speech writers, of military leaders and task-report analysts, advising, steering, and guiding. It has long been so; even Andrew Jackson had his kitchen cabinet. But The Man in the White House is now more than ever the front man of a vast team, the end-product of an expert and highly organised machine that is run in highly professional and costly fashion. We have moved a long way from Washington's and Jefferson's world— Richard Hofstadter described Jefferson as the "Aristocrat as Democrat"—even from the operations of an F. D. Roosevelt—whom he described as the "Patrician as Opportunist"—to a world where all Presidents are not only operators of consensus but are themselves synthetic products, and often indeed are the prisoners of their own images. By 1984 perhaps the profiles of the American leaders, whether of politics or business, will be less profiles than silhouettes.

WASHINGTON
The Man and the Myth[1]

Few figures in American history are so difficult to assess as George Washington. From his first official assignment for Lieutenant-Governor Dinwiddie of Virginia in 1753, until his retirement from the Presidency in 1797, he occupied a central place in the affairs of his country, and for two long spells, in war and then in peace, he held its major office. He became a legend in his own lifetime and a demi-god on his death, which occurred in December 1799. Within five days of his death, Henrietta Liston, the Scots-born wife of British Minister Robert Liston, was writing to her uncle in Glasgow that Washington

> stood the barrier betwixt the Northernmost and South-ernmost States. He was the Unenvied Head of the Army, and such was the magic of his name that his opinion was a sanction equal to law.

Her husband viewed the first birthday celebrations after Washington's death with more detachment

> ... these ceremonies tend to elevate the spirit of the people, and contribute to the formation of a national character, which they consider as much wanting in this country. And ... Americans will be gainers by the periodical recital of the features of their Revolutionary

[1] [Originally published in *History Today*, v (1955), pp. 825-32.]

war and repetition of the praises of Washington—
The hyperbolical amplifications of the Panegyricks in
question have an evident effect, especially among the
younger part of the community, in fomenting the
growth of that Vanity which to the feelings of a stranger
had already arrived at a sufficient height.

Despite Liston's disparagement, it became the practice
to observe Washington's birthday with appropriate orations and ceremonies—indeed, before the Civil War,
the twenty-second of February was, apart from the
Fourth of July, the only genuinely national holiday in
the United States.

Of the 2,200 tracts and publications which were printed
in the United States in 1800, more than 400 were in one
way or another concerned with his death. In America's
most self-consciously republican age, Washington's
image was fixed on the public mind not only by writers
but by artists, by the aloof and patrician portraits of
Gilbert Stuart, and by the canvases of John Trumbull
and Charles Willson Peale. Stuart painted Washington at
least one hundred and twenty-four times. When the
President granted three sittings at Philadelphia in 1795,
four Peales set up their easels around him: Charles,
brother James, and sons Rembrandt, and Raphaelle.
Exhibitions were staged of the Goddess Minerva gazing
upon a bust of Washington, equestrian statues of him
wearing Roman costume were proposed, and Charles
Willson Peale's portrait of him at Trenton, described by
one critic as "just a farmer trying to seem at ease among
the paraphernalia of war", was so popular that some
nineteen variants of it were made. In sculpture, Jean

Antoine Houdon and Horatio Greenough ministered to the hero-worship. If the portraits were stylised, so was the written record. As the public image of him became fixed—the high-booted General in buff and blue, or the impassive statesman at Philadelphia—so did the national legend. The itinerant book-pedlar and ex-parson, Mason Weems, whom Senator Beveridge was later to describe as "part Whitefield, part Villon", invented the hatchet and the cherry tree myth and pictured Washington as a remarkable schoolboy:

> About five years after the death of his father, he quitted school for ever, leaving the boys in tears for his departure; for he had ever lived among them in the spirit of a brother. He was never guilty of so brutish a practice as that of fighting himself; nor would he, when able to prevent it, allow them to fight one another. If he could not disarm their savage passions by his arguments, he would instantly go to the master, and inform him of their barbarous intentions. The boys ... were often angry with George for this—but he used to say "angry or not angry, you shall never, boys, have my consent to a practice so shocking!"

Chief Justice John Marshall's *Life of George Washington* (1804–7) set a pattern for subsequent biographers less human than that of Weems, identifying Washington with national unity, which, for Marshall, meant High Federalism.

The Rev Jared Sparks, who published the first edition of Washington's writings in 1837, did so only after he had carefully vetted and doctored the General's style. Attempts were made, even by the most gifted of his nineteenth-century biographers, Washington Irving (1855-9), to portray him as a good churchgoer, which he was not, and to deny that he married for money, which he did. All dwelt on his courage, his selfless service, his patriotism.

From the repetitions of the countenance—in oil and pastel and miniatures, the etchings and engravings on china plates and glass pitchers—and from the literary variations on the theme of national hero, there emerged a blurred and stilted figure, an icon which not even the bitterness of the Civil War could infuse with life. The cornerstone of the Washington Monument, long a subject of debate, was laid in 1848, and the campaign for subscriptions in the years that followed kept his memory green at a time when both North and South sought to profit by it. To William Cullen Bryant, in a volume of verse published in 1844, Washington was an "elastic chain" binding new states and old in a strong union. Henry Clay of Kentucky, in one of his last speeches, reminded the Senate in 1850 of Washington's paternal warning "to beware of sectional division, to beware of demagogues, to beware of the consequences of indulging a spirit of disunion". Six weeks later, another Senator drew different conclusions. On 4 March, with less than a month of life before him, John C. Calhoun of South Carolina was too weak to address the Senate but was present when James Mason of Virginia—later the Confederate envoy to Britain whose removal from the British Royal Mail Steamer *Trent* by a Northern captain brought Britain close to war with the Union—read for him his last speech on the slavery controversy:

Nor can the Union be saved by invoking the name of that illustrious Southerner whose mortal remains repose on the western bank of the Potomac. He was one of us— a slaveholder and a planter. We have studied his history, and find nothing in it to justify submission to wrong. On the contrary, his great fame rests on the solid foundation, that while he was careful to avoid doing wrong to others, he was prompt and decided in repelling wrong. I trust that in this respect, we profited by his example.

Not all Southerners agreed. It was a Southern woman, Ann Pamela Cunningham, who in 1853 began the movement which produced the Mount Vernon Ladies' Association of the Union, and on Washington's Birthday in 1859 his home was bought for preservation as a national shrine. It was for this cause that Edward Everett, the greatest orator of his day, toured the country and between 1856 and 1860 delivered the most famous of all Washington's Birthday orations, "The Character of Washington", no less than 129 times. The unveiling in Richmond of the equestrian statue of him was made the occasion in 1858 for further appeals for national unity by Virginia's Governor Wise and Senator Robert Hunter. In 1860 Everett published his own life of Washington. This life was read in January 1861 by Lieutenant-Colonel Robert E. Lee, stationed at Fort Mason, Texas. Writing to his family, at a moment when he still thought that the conflict might be averted, Lee lamented the situation: "How his (Washington's) spirit would be grieved could he see the wreck of his mighty labors!" For Lee it was a moment of miserable decision. He was steeped in the Washington tradition, for Washington had been his

father's friend; his father's funeral oration before the two
Houses of Congress—"first in war, first in peace, and
first in the hearts of his countrymen"—had contributed to
the growth of the legend; Lee's wife, Mary Custis, was a
great-granddaughter of Martha Washington; his estate,
Arlington on the Potomac, up river from Mount Vernon,
had been bought by Martha's son, and Arlington House
had been built by Martha's grandson and named after
an older Custis property on the Virginian Eastern shore.
When, some years later, writing to Beauregard, Lee
expressed the opinion that patriotism might require a
man seemingly to reverse his principles, the example he
cited was that of Washington, fighting at one time for
the King, later commanding the forces against him. And
Washington was above reproach, at once the symbol of
successful and legitimate rebellion, and of national union.
Significantly, the building of the Washington Monument
was halted by the war. It was not resumed until Reconstruction was over.

Through the rest of the century, the pattern held. To
Henry Cabot Lodge, Ph.D., Harvard, and later Massa-
chusetts Senator, who published his own biography of
Washington in 1895, there was significance in "the stream
of praise". "The opinion of the world, however reached,
becomes in the course of years or centuries the nearest
approach we can make to final judgment on things
human. . . . When years after his death the world agrees
to call a man great, the verdict must be accepted."
Washington, he thought, stood alone, "above conflict and
superior to malice", a type. "Whether the image be true
or false is of no consequence: the fact endures." But, to

offset these uncritical assumptions, Lodge recognised that the picture of Washington had become largely mythical and echoed McMaster's words: "General Washington is known to us, and President Washington. But George Washington is an unknown man."

He did not remain so much longer. The New History, the socio-economic school of James Harvey Robinson and Harry Elmer Barnes, brought a social criticism to bear on the writing of American history, and Charles Beard looked at the Constitution with the eyes of an economic determinist. There were not only new vantage points, there were improved techniques, and there was more abundant evidence—by 1932 the Bicentennial Commission began to make Washington's writings available, and there came full editions of other Revolutionary papers, and of the writings of his colleagues and contemporaries. The result was a swing of the pendulum, from iconography to something like iconoclasm, from hero-worship almost to desecration. In 1926 the first volume appeared of Rupert Hughes' three-volume study, followed by other examples of the humanising and debunking school. They reflected, like Lytton Strachey in Britain, less the satisfaction of men discovering new facts about former periods than the disillusion of men with their own times. Like Strachey, in his studies of Victorianism, they aimed their arrows at the key-figure in the Revolutionary period, and they sought to make of him a figurehead. And like him, they took as their axiom the words of a Master—"Je n'impose rien; je ne propose rien; j'expose." Washington, it was discovered, had used stronger language to General Charles Lee at the

Battle of Monmouth than either Weems or Sparks would have liked—or printed. Washington had enemies, and attempts had been made to replace him as Commander-in-Chief during the war. Washington, in any event, had made mistakes as a commander, on the Indian frontier in 1754 and during the Revolutionary struggle itself. Washington crossed the Delaware, yes, but his retreat across the Jerseys before that was an inglorious story. He was not always in control of his temper, or of his aides at headquarters. He had, moreover, written a letter to Sally Fairfax, wife of his mentor, neighbour, and best friend, which hinted at feelings that went suspiciously beyond the boundary of friendship. Writing in 1934, Professor N. W. Stephenson summed up the new orientation, at the beginning of a delightful commentary on Rupert Hughes' volume in the *American Historical Review*, when he said that of late years certain romantic biographers had made a sentimental discovery about Washington. "They phrase it by saying that they have proved him to be a 'human being'. What they mean is that they believe he was in love with his neighbour's wife." Today the pendulum appears to be swinging back to what is—though for how long?—a central position. In the great study of Washington that he unhappily did not live to complete, Douglas Southall Freeman used the mass of evidence now available on Washington, his State and his times, sifted it with care and with affection, and provided, if not the rounded picture of the man, yet the most thorough and objective biography of him yet written. Unlike Lytton Strachey, he did not believe that "ignorance is the first requisite of the historian—

ignorance, which simplifies and clarifies, which selects
and omits". Freeman recognised that it was ignorance and
unavailability of the sources that had allowed the legends
to grow, and that only in detailed knowledge lay the
truth about Washington and his times.

This is not to say that problems and difficulties no
longer remain. Granting the legend, why did it begin?
The Washington apotheosis took place in an Age of
Reason, dedicated to a strictly rationalistic and natural-
istic view of mankind; an age, too, of pamphlet wars and
pamphleteers, ready to use the most tenuous charges to
blacken a reputation—witness the activities in the first
decade of American history of Freneau and Cobbett, of
Callender and William Duane. Why were Washington's
defeats and misjudgments and explosions of temper so
much more sympathetically treated than the blunders of
others? Why, later, when he began to move into a party
camp, was he so much less criticised than others?—for,
if not exempt from attack, he never received the insults
that were heaped on Jefferson and Adams, Burr and
Hamilton. How did the popular opinion of him, the
affection and trust, emerge through the barriers of dis-
tance and of etiquette that surrounded him, and to which
he was in any case addicted? How far was the popular
legend accepted by his closest associates, how far used by
them for their own purposes? How far in fact did
Washington as a person come to be politically exploited
before his death as well as after it? And was he ever aware
that he was being exploited? These are the questions
that challenge the modern historian of the Revolutionary period. The answers to these questions will not be

A.P.—C

found by any means fully revealed in Washington's own writings.

Unlike Franklin or Jefferson, and to a lesser degree Hamilton and Madison, Washington did not speak in aphorisms, and his writings, brief letters for the most part on specific problems, are conspicuously lacking in those statements of general ideas and objectives to which his contemporaries were so addicted. Unlike them, he did not enjoy writing, and until the Farewell Address in 1796, he wrote nothing of a sustained or systematic nature. There is little in the way of personal comment and reminiscence, and still less of gossip and autobiography. His letters have the tone rather of situation reports. He did not write for posterity, but he was fully aware that his papers would be precious material for later historians, and, as with his daily life, they were ordered and arranged with care. But they lack the sense of unity and spontaneity that Jefferson's possess, the reflexion of a characteristic temper of mind, the eighteenth-century belief in the "universals" that the world was intelligible and orderly and a product of a natural law. What system Washington's correspondence possesses is provided by the world about him, rather than by any inner philosophy of life. His letters relate to action, to the practical and the tangible, and one has to know the whole situation into which they fit to understand them. To this, not unusual, difficulty in the correspondence of a busy and anxious man has to be added the restraint induced in one who was naturally cautious by the Revolutionary War. Unflattering comments and news of military value would be dangerous instruments if they fell into British hands;

many letters were drafted by his aides and put in a formal
style; as his own significance grew during the War,
caution grew with it. And the more he became identified
with the Revolution, the more the private person became
merged in the public figure. This was inevitable and
deliberate. He became elusive, remote, enigmatic. As it
was to be later with Lee, so with Washington:

> . . . And so we get the marble man again,
> The head on the Greek coin, the idol-image,
> Worshipped, uncomprehended and aloof,
> A figure lost to flesh and blood and bones,
> Frozen into a legend out of life,
> A blank-verse statue.

What, however, a reading of Washington's correspondence does reveal is the constancy of the man's character,
his unquestioning devotion to the cause once he had
chosen it, and—what struck his colleagues and compatriots so forcibly—his refusal to countenance any
suggestions of usurpation of authority by others, or by
himself. The twentieth century is perhaps better able to
appreciate the appeal of such integrity than the nineteenth, with its happy sense, despite the Civil War, of the
automatic triumph of constitutional principles. To the
eighteenth century a military leader who knew when to
withdraw, whose ambition was so closely linked to his
country's cause that it never became self-aggrandisement
or tyranny, was a hero indeed. It was this rather than his
skill in the field that established his reputation. He was
not regarded, by others or by himself, as a great strategist.
Until he became Commander-in-Chief he had never
commanded more than a regiment. It was Greene and

Gates and Lee, Montgomery (until his death) and
Arnold (until his treason) who earned the laurels. But
Washington was pre-eminently fitted to handle the
business of war: he was an excellent organiser in an army
that lacked a professional staff; he was self-reliant; if he
had doubts he had learnt when and where not to reveal
them; he was physically strong and physically impressive, a superb horseman in an age when it mattered;
he was a disciplinarian with no hesitations about the lash.
He had the qualities of command without the menace of
overweening ambition. The root of his triumph in war
and his skill in peace was this integrity. And he knew it.
On 19 Jun. 1775, four days after his election to command
the Continental Army, he said:

> I can answer but for three things, a firm belief in the
> justice of our Cause, close attention in the prosecution
> of it, and the strictest integrity.

By 1778 he had succeeded, as no one else could have
done, in keeping the Army intact, in holding public
opinion true to the cause, and in placating—and getting
all too few supplies from—Congress. If he was not the
architect of victory, he alone made the victory possible.
His work after 1783 was much more important than his
work before it, but without his services and his reputation
not only would the cause have faltered, the man who led
would have been a different being. The trust put in him
was in the end a tribute to his character.

This is something which—by contrast—perhaps the
eighteenth and nineteenth centuries understood in a way
the twentieth does not. It is not that the twentieth does

not respect character, but it finds the eighteenth-century concept of it more difficult to grasp than, say, Jefferson's eloquence or Hamilton's financial tactics. For the eighteenth century believed that character could be formed, by self-discipline and control, as Washington's was formed. Whereas in our own age control and discipline are held to be psychologically frustrating, and a premium is put on spontaneity, in the eighteenth century character and manners were deliberately and self-consciously cultivated; and concern with one's position and one's reputation was regarded with respect, and not with shame. Washington was in this sense a self-made man; he greatly valued the esteem in which he was held, for he had set out quite avowedly to win it.

A legend, then, even before his death; a dim and somewhat dehumanised figure, whose writings and speeches when they were printed suggested a cold and reserved man, cautious and canny, preoccupied with the opinion others might hold of him in his lifetime and afterwards, preoccupied with what he called his "honour". Is this the real Washington? Have the labours of recent years, and particularly the researches of Fitzpatrick and of Freeman, revealed a warmer, a less stilted figure? Freeman's death before he had grappled with the problems of the second term was a sad loss to scholarship, for the most intriguing problem that Washington's career now poses for historians is not "Why was he successful?" or even "Why was he so greatly venerated?" but "What was his role as President and 'Chief'?" This is a crucial problem, for every decision he made, however trivial, set a precedent for his successors, as he fully recognised. The answers Washington found for the issues of foreign policy, on tax and tariff questions, for the problems of the Indians or the farmers, these set a pattern not only for his party but for his country, and some of the patterns held for more than a century. American history was given direction and shape by the decisions of Washington's two terms and by the Presidency of John Adams. The satisfaction to be derived from a study of his career rests, on the other hand, in the realisation that in times of crisis it is not learning so much as character that counts—judgment, reliability, and integrity. That Washington had deliberately schooled himself into becoming the man he was did not weaken his appeal to the men of the eighteenth century nor minimise his contribution to the victory of the United States in rebellion and her survival in peace.

BENJAMIN FRANKLIN
A Tradesman in the Age of Reason[1]

Benjamin Franklin, to his contemporaries the greatest figure America had yet produced, was born in January 1706. Publisher, printer, essayist and author, scientist, philologist, politician, "General", diplomat, Fellow of the Royal Society, Doctor of Laws of Oxford and St Andrews, federalist, though not in a party sense, in all the roles he played he remained still very much himself. In his range, his origins, his success, Franklin seemed to be the living answer to Hector St John de Crèvecoeur's famous question in 1784, "What then *is* the American, this new man?" David Hume thought Franklin "the first philosopher, and indeed the first great man of letters for whom we are beholden to America". Some of his own compatriots bracketed him with Washington, but honest, splenetic John Adams wrote, rather spitefully, to Dr Rush,

> The history of our Revolution will be one continued lie from one end to the other. The essence of the whole will be that Dr Franklin's electrical rod smote the earth and out sprang General Washington. That Franklin electrified him with his rod, and thenceforward these two conducted all the policy, negotiations, legislatures, and war.

[1] [Originally published in *History Today*, VI (1956), pp. 439-47.]

He admitted Franklin's genius, original, sagacious, inventive, but he could not see where his excellence lay as legislator or as politician or as negotiator. "From day to day he sat in silence at the Continental Congress," he said, "a great part of his time fast asleep in his chair", and in France he was too self-indulgent to attend regularly to the business of the embassy.

Later biographers have described him in more kindly terms and in a variety of ways—*Franklin, the Apostle of Modern Times*, Father of American Democracy, The Many-Sided Franklin, Socrates at the Printing Press, Father of American Ingenuity, The first high priest of the religion of efficiency, or even *Franklin, the First Civilised American*. For Franklin's success was striking. Born with no advantages, he helped to unite his newly independent country, and to conclude an alliance with France which greatly contributed to American victory in 1783; he became a lion in the literary world of Paris; and he acted as conciliator at large and Founding Father Extraordinary in the debates over the Constitution at Philadelphia in 1787. Yet, despite services almost as great as Washington's, references to him in academic circles in the United States were greeted, until recently at least, with a denigrating smile and a raised eyebrow. Where then does Franklin's reputation stand one quarter of a millenium after his birth?

Franklin's very versatility is suspect in our own more specialist age. In the eighteenth century it was still possible for a man to take all learning to be his province; easier in America than in Europe, and easier there to earn the reputation, like Jefferson, of being a man of parts.

Today this catholic range is discredited; Franklin's scientific experiments, his identification of electricity and lightning, his study of solar heat, of ocean currents, of the causes of storms, his interest in population studies and statistics are dismissed as the amateur dabblings of a superficial scientist.

There is more abundant cause for the raising of eyebrows. Franklin was born, unsuitably as it proved, in Puritan Boston, the tenth son and seventeenth child of a tallow chandler and soap boiler who had emigrated from Northampton, and baptised in Boston's Old South Church. Despite this favourable beginning, his youthful character was not all that it might have been. He was apprenticed to an elder brother, a printer, but relations were never harmonious; he became as egotistical as he was precocious—as an old man looking back on the past he told his son, "I do not remember when I could not read". He ran away to distant Philadelphia; he embezzled money; he had an illegitimate son William, born in the same year as the father was attempting a literary work called *The Art of Virtue*, a son of whom he was very fond, but who later became, through Bute's influence, Governor of New Jersey and a royalist, and later still, himself the father of an illegitimate son. Franklin never lost his interest in women; Cobbett, at the time a bitter Federalist pamphleteer in Philadelphia, could refer to him seven years after his death as "a crafty and lecherous old hypocrite ... whose very statue seems to gloat on the wenches as they walk the State House yard". If never vain, he was certainly not untouched by flattery, in Philadelphia or France. He remained a racy and roguish figure to the end, and rarely chose to hide his indiscretions. It is not a picture to everyone's taste, and the distaste is increased by Franklin's sententiousness, his proneness to give advice—much sought, especially when, over seventy, he was the most popular man in Paris. La Rochefoucauld's maxim of a century before—"Old men are fond of giving good advice, because they are no longer in a position to set bad examples"—applies all too aptly.

Perhaps what is at the root of this distaste is the difficulty our own century finds in understanding the pre-occupation of the eighteenth century with personal success and reputation, and in understanding the eighteenth-century American view of character and behaviour. In our own day, living in crowded cities and faced with the menace of routine and mechanical processes, we have put an emphasis on spontaneity, on a man's native gifts for life, on untrammelled self-expression. Eighteenth-century Americans would have regarded this as naïve, for they had no illusions about the need for discipline, or about the motives that drove men to seek success and influence. Indeed what the colonial frontier taught was that either you learn to discipline yourself or you die. To lose patience with the elements in a rough sea off Cape Cod, or with Indians on the forest trails of the Alleghenies, was to lose your life. America bred political freedom, but in practical matters it bred caution and patience, judgment and discretion, tolerance and *finesse*, and it was on these qualities that successful careers were built. Americans then strove as much for self-restraint and self-mastery as for self-government. Witness the career of Washington on the one hand, and his concern with what he called his "honour"; witness the observations of Paine and Jefferson on the other. However divided on matters of political interpretation they might be, all would have shared a common respect for the qualities of discipline and balance; all recognised in their own natures how their instincts had to be curbed by reason. Reputations were made the hard way by deliberate character-training. Witness again Washington's laborious Rules of Civility, the hundred or more rules by which social success might be achieved. There are obvious parallels here with Boswell and Rousseau and Lord Chesterfield.

When Benjamin Franklin devised *Poor Richard* and used him as a vehicle of exhortation and advice—and when from time to time he revealed how hard self-control was for himself—his fellows knew what he meant. He was a practical man, writing in his annual periodical *Poor Richard's Almanac*, for other practical men. Frankly-recognised natural instincts should, indeed must, be harnessed, if a reputation was to be made and merited. And this, the self-reliance that originated as a frontier gospel, became the key doctrine of American Transcendentalism. Franklin's disciple is Emerson, as Carlyle saw; if Emerson rejected Franklin's man because "he savoured of nothing heroic", *Poor Richard* still lives on, with sanctity added to sanctimoniousness, in the pages of *The Journals*. In the *Almanac* Franklin printed common-sense observations and wise saws, culled mainly from Rabelais and Swift and Sterne—and he did not pretend to originality. He made it, in fact, the first great syndicated column in American journalism. He wrote with unerring skill and great charm for the colonial equivalent of the man in the street, in this case the man on the farm and on the frontier. He wrote easily on half a hundred topics —*Dissertation on Liberty and Necessity, Pleasure and Pain, The Way to Wealth, On the Causes and Cure of Smoky Chimneys*. He became a folk-philosopher, sharper than Confucius, more ruminative than Dale Carnegie. The middle-class morality, which Shaw and D. H. Lawrence pilloried but which is still at the vital roots of American prosperity, and which is reflected in its industry, its native shrewdness, its frugality, its practicality, can be said to find its first prophet in Benjamin Franklin, though no one would have enjoyed Shaw's criticisms or Lawrence's virility more than Franklin. He confessed with gusto that he practised the frugality he preached just as long as poverty forced him to—and not a moment longer.

Poor Richard has been regarded by many as the mentor of early American capitalism. His advice is certainly keyed to the two notes: work hard and count your pennies: the sleeping Fox catches no poultry; then plough deep, while Sluggards sleep, and you shall have Corn to sell and to keep; what maintains one Vice, would bring up two children;

> Many Estates are spent on the Getting
> Since Women for Tea forsook Spinning and Knitting
> And Men for Punch forsook Hewing and Splitting.

Not that all *Poor Richard*'s moralities were exhortations to enterprise. Some were of an earthier sort: a single man is like the odd half of a pair of scissors; he that takes a wife takes care; keep your eyes wide open before marriage, half shut afterwards; you cannot pluck roses without fear of thorns, nor enjoy a fair wife without danger of horns. But in nothing is Franklin more typical of his century and of his country than in his insistence that self-reliance and hard work are basic to liberty. He believed in free speech, free goods, and free men. He opposed the efforts of all exploiters, whether merchants in England, Scotch factors in America, landowners or priests, to restrain man's natural freedoms. And freedom, he argued, paid. Printers, he said, in his characteristically deflated way

> are educated in the Belief, that when Men differ in Opinion, both sides ought equally to have the advantage of being heard by the Publick; and that when Truth and Error have Fair Play, the former is always an over-match for the latter: Hence they chearfully serve all contending Writers that pay them well, without regarding on which side they are of the Question in Dispute ...

Certainly his *Almanac* sold: ten thousand copies a year before long. "I grew in a little time", he said, "expert at selling". And though he did not mention it, expert at buying. He set up eighteen paper mills, purchased rags for them, and took the paper they made, either using it himself or selling it to other printing houses. As Professor Bridenbaugh has shown in his study of *The Colonial Craftsman*, "it is extremely doubtful if any Englishman was as large a paper dealer as *Poor Richard* in these years". And he quickly realised that one source of the successful salesmanship was his own reputation.

> In order to secure my credit and character as a trades-man, I took care not only to be in *reality* industrious and frugal, but to avoid all *appearances* of the contrary. I dressed plain and was seen at no places of idle diversion. I never went out a fishing or shooting; a book, indeed, sometimes debauched me from my work, but that was seldom, snug and gave no scandal. ... Thus being esteemed an industrious, thriving young man, and paying duly for what I bought ... I went on swim-mingly.

If this sounds like the wiliness of Mr Pepys in the language of Mr Pooter, it could be paralleled by similar, if less frank, reflexions in the Papers of many a contemporary, George Washington included. In a sense all the Revolu-tionaries were self-made men, and some of them in making their reputations made a Revolution. The Yankee virtues triumphed not at Appomattox but at Yorktown.

It is true that there were contemporaries too who were not attracted by Franklin's sentiments. They never won much approval in the American South, with its open-handed ways, its code of the gentleman, its aversion from trade; and they were anathema to many in Boston. But to Carlyle, and many since his day, Ben Franklin has become "the Father of all the Yankees". To many even outside the Southern States, Yankee is an opprobrious term, a badge of trade and a badge of infamy, yet it was these Yankee values that were transforming the eighteenth-century world. Both Boston and Virginia, in their different ways, were aristocratic: names and con-nexions counted. Franklin lived by trade, prospered by it and was acclaimed across the world. He was completely and avowedly bourgeois, happy in the company of men, and women too, efficient in keeping a contract, adept at conciliation and in the affairs of towns. Virginian Jefferson was afraid of towns as threats to the rural democracy he worked for; Franklin, though he presented himself to the French as a backwoodsman, was only at ease when he was in them. He transformed Philadelphia. To him it owed the fact that it had a city police, the paved and lighted streets that were the surprise of Virginians and New Englanders. To him, too, it owed the American Philosophical Society and the University of Pennsylvania and the first circulating library in America. To him the country—before it had yet been born—owed the efficiency of its postal service, and its first project of a Federation. His Junto might be called the first collection of Rotarians in history, "seeking the promotion of our interests in business by more extensive recommendation". Versatile, businesslike, complaisant by disposition, Franklin strikes a modern note, the first of the joiners and boosters and glad-handers. Well might William Green call him the Patron Saint of Labour, in his practice and preaching of diligence, thrift, caution, his faith that good causes could be linked to self-advancement, that sweet reasonableness did not prevent a good conceit of oneself. But this doctrine too is out of favour. Hard work and thrift are no longer held to be unquestioned guarantees of success either in Britain or in America. As the *New York Times* put it as long ago as 1938, "*Poor Richard* appeals now only to vulgar minds. . . . Why count the pennies when millions of dollars are pouring out from the

inexhaustible Federal Horn of Plenty?" It was easier in
Franklin's day than in Franklin Roosevelt's to make a
case for his Industrious Apprentice.

History, then, has not been very sympathetic to his
reputation or to his doctrine. Nor has it dealt very kindly
with his political services to the American Revolution.
It has become very clear that in his days as a Colonial
Agent in London he was working not for the independence of the colonies but for a form of Federal Union. He
disapproved of the Boston Tea Party and, until his
return to America in 1775, his journalism was much less
influential than that of Sam Adams. He admired England,
he enjoyed London society, he deprecated violence.
And even his services in France are open to question. If
one argues that the French Alliance was vital to American
success in the Revolution, one must admit Franklin's
services: yet French troops, money, arms, and commercial privileges were coming through, thanks to
Beaumarchais, in secret but abundantly, long before the
treaty was signed. It was perhaps the quick loss of New
York which checked French intervention as early as 1776.
The signing of the Alliance after Saratoga suggests that
Vergennes was influenced less by emissaries in Paris than
by events in America. And the picture, also, of the
homespun patriot at the bar of the Commons in 1765,
and that of the fur-capped philosopher at Versailles, the
toast of French society, is one that makes little appeal to
an age suspicious of histrionics.

Yet this is to deny his diplomatic services—and they
were not confined to his years abroad. If as a Colonial
Agent he worked for compromise, he worked for it all his

The Toast of French Society, "Au genie de Franklin".
Allegorical engraving by Fragonard.

Portrait of Alexander Hamilton by John Trumbull.

life. Standing at the bar of the House, he told the Commons in 1765 that "every assembly on the American continent, and every member in every assembly" had denied Parliament's authority to pass the Stamp Act. As Deputy Postmaster-General of North America he was himself an example of emerging colonial unity. As plain Ben Franklin, large, broad-shouldered, with his big head and square deft hands, self-taught and practical, he was the embodiment of the colonial protest, "the ultimate Whig". In France from 1776 these qualities were held in still higher regard: to Vergennes he was an instrument of French imperial revenge on Britain, to the Encyclopaedists and Physiocrats a natural man from a republican wilderness, to blue stockings a rustic philosopher with civilised tastes, with an approving eye for the ladies and a neat democratic wit. In Paris and in Passy, he was surrounded by an admiring court. His French, no more than passable, seemed charming. His portrait appeared on medallions, rings, and snuff boxes. To all Franklin was a proof of republican simplicity and virtue; he was the American, this new man. The fur cap was worn to hide his eczema; it was mistaken for a badge of the frontier. Since he was cast in the role of wise and simple philosopher he played the part. He could be Solon and Silenus, gallant and Gallic, to suit all tastes, and not least his own.

In his years in France he showed an uncanny diplomatic skill. He used the same facility in his last great work at the Federal Convention in 1787. In his *Autobiography* he has left a description of diplomatic technique around the conference table from which we can still learn:

A.P.—D

I made it a rule to forbear all direct contradiction to the sentiments of others and all positive assertion of my own. I even forbade myself . . . the use of every word or expression in the language that imported a fixed opinion such as "certainly", "undoubtedly", etc.; and I adopted instead of them "I conceive", "I apprehend" or "I imagine" a thing to be so or so, or "It so appears to me at present". When another asserted something that I thought an error, I denied myself the pleasure of contradicting him abruptly and of showing immediately some absurdity in his proposition; and in answering I began by observing that in certain cases or circumstances his opinion would be right, but that in the present case there "appeared" or "seemed to me" some difference, etc. I soon found the advantage of this change . . .

And if he fought for colonial rights and understanding in London in 1765, he was still fighting for tolerance and the other point of view in 1787. The speech that James Wilson delivered for him on the last day of the Convention—he was too old and too infirm to stand—was the product of long experience and expressed that reasonableness that the twentieth century as well as the eighteenth might regard as the closest approximation that finite man can make to wisdom. He appealed to his colleagues among the Founding Fathers who opposed the Constitution to doubt with himself a little of their own infallibility. I confess, he said, that

I do not entirely approve of this Constitution at present, but Sir, I am not sure I shall never approve it: For having lived long, I have experienced many instances

of being obliged, by better information or fuller consideration to change opinion even on important subjects,
which I once thought right, but found to be otherwise.
It is therefore that the older I grow the more apt I am to
doubt my own judgment, and to pay more respect to the
judgment of others ... I consent, Sir, to this Constitution, because I expect no better, and because I am not
sure that it is not the best. The opinions I have had of
its errors I sacrifice to the public good. I have never
whisper'd a syllable of them abroad. Within these walls
they were born, and here they shall die.

One can understand the doubts that have over the last
century attached to Franklin's reputation, both personal
and political. He was not, like Washington or Jefferson, a
Virginian landowner devoting himself to public affairs,
and he has been harder to fit into a nationalist mythology.
When in 1788 he drew up his will, he began "I, Benjamin
Franklin, of Philadelphia, printer, late Minister Pleni-
potentiary from the United States of America to the
Court of France, now President of the State of Pennsylvania." There is a ring of triumph about it, but it is a
bourgeois triumph, the success is not sublime but smug.
And the sentiments would be repeated, indeed from 1828
would become part of the American political creed. In
1840:

> Old Tip he wears a homespun coat
> He has no ruffled shirt, wirt, wirt,
> If Mat has all the golden plate
> He is a little squirt, wirt, wirt.

In 1861 "From log cabin to White House", in 1940, "I
came up the hard way". Dixon Wecter once likened

Franklin to a Sancho Panza, "rejoicing in homely wisdom, thinking of belly and pocket-book as he ambles by the side of the greater idealist, the godlike Washington". The fact was that Franklin was infinitely more symbolic, infinitely more dangerous, infinitely more modern-minded, than Washington. And in the contemporary assessments of him there is not a little fear. He was so adept, riches seemed to come his way so smoothly, he left his grandson a fortune of five hundred thousand dollars, he won the plaudits of foreigners. John Adams, always jealous of the affection of the French for Franklin, seemed to think he had caused the French Revolution. "The best talents in France were blind disciples of Franklin and Turgot, and led the blind to destruction."

Of the fathers of his country, whatever the years might have done to his reputation, Franklin is perhaps the most significant, the most cosmopolitan, the most prescient for the future, the new man. The printer had made himself the first specimen Yankee. He was a successful tradesman in an age of reason, his *Autobiography* is the first American self-revelation of a self-made man. By his *Almanac* and by his career he preached the American faith: reliance on oneself and on one's own efforts, prudence, good sense, and the respect of one's neighbours. Like Jefferson he saw no limits to the capacity of free men, as citizens, as workers or as liberal enquirers after truth in many fields. Like Jefferson again, he was a deist. During his years in England, he undertook along with Sir Francis Dashwood a revision of the Prayer Book, and of the Catechism he retained only two questions: "What is your duty to God?" and "What is your duty to your neighbour?" Franklin's faith in political freedom was linked to a faith in economic freedom, and to a faith in scientific freedom, too. He ranged widely and he ranged easily: there is no sense of superiority, rather the reverse, but there is certainly an effortlessness that comes not from Balliol or Boston but from a confidence in the capacity of what he called "the middling people". Franklin learnt by reading and by observation, and what he learnt he sought to apply. The test was empirical, and the tests were endless. Human, gregarious, worldly, enquiring yet unspeculative, restless yet equable in temper, unpompous, a preacher of moralities who honoured them as much in the breach as in the observance, a counsellor of prudence who was always ready to take a chance, a plain man who liked the graces and the comforts of life, a master of slogans who never deceived himself by them, sceptic and idealist and a lover of children, he has left his mark conspicuously on the American character. He was father of all the Yankees, perhaps—for did not *Poor Richard* say "The cat in gloves catches no mice?"—but ambassador also to two great kingdoms. His worldly wisdom was suited to the *philosophes* in Paris and in Edinburgh; it was suited, too, to the old wives in the chimney corner, summing up a lifetime of neighbourly experience. He was at home in France. In England, he said, he was thought of as too much of an American, and in America was deemed too much an Englishman. He was rightly thought of as a citizen of the world, and this, too, is part of his legacy to Americans. He wrote his own epitaph, perhaps the most famous of all American epitaphs:

The Body of B. Franklin, Printer, (Like the Cover of an old Book, Its Contents torn out and Stript of its Lettering and Gilding) Lies here, food for Worms. But the Work shall not be lost; For it will (as he believ'd), appear once more, in a new and more elegant Edition, Revised and Corrected, by the Author.

ALEXANDER HAMILTON[1]
Founding Father

The decade from 1790 to 1800 in American history remains largely *terra incognita*. While other periods, especially the Revolution and the Civil War, have been chronicled abundantly, the first years of the Republic remain clouded and its citizens shadowy beings—unless, in their own lifetimes, they were seen to be "demi-gods". Franklin was so seen, to his amusement; Washington, to his embarrassment. But this process of "amplification", largely the work of Weems and Marshall, Gilbert Stuart and the Peales, was highly selective.

The mythology and hero-worship inseparable from nation-building are of course largely fortuitous. Soldiers are preferred to "organisers of victory", adventurers to politicians and financiers; simple men of action make better symbols than the complex and the paradoxical. Yet, in any reckoning, the indifference shown by American historians to Alexander Hamilton, and to the drama of his career, is astonishing.

A man of effervescent charm, short in stature, but fair and "uncommonly handsome"; a West Indian immigrant working his way through college, who made the Revolutionary cause his own; for more than four years "first aid" to the Commander-in-Chief, as the Spanish envoy happily described him, and a fighting

[1] [Originally published in *History Today*, VII (1957), pp. 182-9.]

soldier with Lafayette at Yorktown; joint author with Madison of the Constitution and of *The Federalist*, the eighty-five essays which, more perhaps than anything else, secured the adoption of the Constitution in New York; "prime minister" to the first President; Secretary of the Treasury, whose report on credit and whose banking policies established the solvency and set the course of the new state; major contributor to Washington's Farewell Address and thus to the shaping of American foreign policy for the next century; a meteor that swept across the political scene and whose brilliance was so dramatically extinguished: why has Hamilton's personality left so little mark?

Was it that his point of view, often so arrogantly voiced, was distasteful and even alien?—"your people, Sir, is a great beast". Was his confidence in himself, so well-justified, nevertheless too extravagant, his capacity for work too overpowering, his long and masterly essays, written almost without pause or need of correction, too persuasive for the man himself to be accepted, much less loved? Was his integrity itself too lofty and too conspicuous, his devotion to the new nation a shade exotic? Or did he merely die too early, cut off before he was fifty by Aaron Burr's pistol shot? Yet his work was done four or even eight years before. And the end was surely in itself material for legend—his life sacrificed in part for the sake of the Union, his devoted wife and large family destitute, his murderer a hunted fugitive with his schemes for secession largely destroyed. His death proved good business for John Trumbull, who was kept profitably employed for years turning out replicas of his

Hamilton portraits. Yet the legend never came to birth, hard though his family tried to induce it.

The success of Hamilton's work deepens the mystery of the failure of his reputation. He fought for, and secured, the funding of the national debt, irrespective of the question of its ownership, at a time when the great majority of Congressmen expected it to be scaled down.[2] This led to a split between Hamilton and Madison, and fostered the growth of parties: but it tied the rich and adventurous to the new state. He secured also the assumption by the Federal Government of the debts of the states; and this step, even more bitterly fought over, enabled the Federal Government to dominate the revenue sources of the country and greatly consolidated national authority. He established a Bank in which the government owned stock; and, when Jefferson objected that the Constitution did not permit this, he answered with the famous doctrine of implied powers—that the power to charter private corporations or a bank was a natural outcome of the power to coin money, raise taxes, and incur debts. He provided a national revenue by imposing indirect taxes on imported goods and an excise tax on home-produced liquor—two measures of profound significance; for the first demanded a high volume of imports from Britain and so linked the United States with her economically and diplomatically, and the second produced the Whisky Rebellion of the Pennsylvania farmers in 1794. Hamilton's vehement suppression of this was designed as a display of national strength.

[2] Edward Channing, *A History of the United States*, 6 vols. N.Y. (1905-32), IV, p. 69.

These measures can be criticised, for they divided the country sectionally and politically. But few American historians have criticised the programme of 1791–4: it has been for the most part praised as inspired and percipient; as giving prestige to American currency; as assuring national stability and the supremacy of the propertied classes; as making for close relations with Britain and as providing a base for the steady expansion of the role of the Federal Government. It has been assessed less on financial than on political grounds, as Hamilton intended it should. For his intentions were primarily political, even imperial.

> A fully negotiable funded debt, drained originally from the small-property classes and met by taxes paid by the masses, was to be used by an emerging moneyed class to create profitable speculative enterprises in lands, industry and finance.[3]

At a time when few dared to tackle the economic problems of a bankrupt and agrarian society, a clear direction was given to the new nation and an "energy to government", in Hamilton's own phrase, as well as "Order to the finances". And they were imposed from above. Hamilton, in 1791 as in 1787, advocated republicanism but not democracy.

> All communities divide themselves into the few and the many. The first are rich and well-born, the other the mass of the people. The voice of the people has been

[3] Rexford Guy Tugwell and Joseph Dorfman, "Alexander Hamilton: Nation-maker", *Columbia University Quarterly*, xxx (1938) p. 64.

> said to be the voice of God; and however generally this maxim has been quoted and believed, it is not true in fact. The people are turbulent and changing; they seldom judge or determine right.[4]

The sentiments, like the financial policy, proved peculiarly useful to nineteenth-century America. They seemed prophetic when Carnegie and Rockefeller appeared; and Lincoln's Republicanism was soon subverted into Hamiltonianism, although then, as now, the imagery was of Illinois rather than New York; the log-cabin is still preferred to "The Grange", homespun, even coon-skin, to Hamilton's white waistcoat and black silk small clothes. Although the language was of *laissez-faire*, enterprise was abetted by high tariffs and railway subsidies. The Fourteenth Amendment abolishing slavery was twisted into a defence not of Negroes but of big business. Grover Cleveland, the only Democrat in the White House from 1860 to 1912, appealed to businessmen to participate actively in politics. The young Virginian Democrat, Woodrow Wilson, proclaimed in 1889: "Ever since I have had independent judgements of my own I have been a Federalist." This was the America with which Joseph Chamberlain had sympathy; F. S. Oliver's essay of 1906, the only English biography of Hamilton, sought in High Federalism the solution to Britain's own Imperial problems.[5]

It is true that Beard, Bryan, Populists, and muck-rakers voiced other opinions: but not all Beard's research could impugn Hamilton's own motives and integrity, or

[4] *Works*, ed. Lodge, i, p. 401.
[5] F. S. Oliver, *Alexander Hamilton, an essay on American Union* (1906).

deny his achievement as architect of Federalism. In the boom-years of the nineteen-twenties, Hamilton's name, coupled with Andrew Mellon's, was on everyone's lips. In the gloom of the thirties Hamilton's stock was still high, when Mellon's was not, as the assessments of Tugwell and Dorfman reveal. In 1934, when Hamilton's Papers on Public Credit, Commerce, and Finance were re-published by the Columbia University Press, they were described by Elihu Root in his foreword as "the lucid and powerful expositions of controlling principles . . . the guide by which our nation has become great and respected . . . as applicable now as they were then". In 1947 as radical a critic as Louis Hacker declared that Hamilton's reading of his times and of the future of America "was that of the wise statesman".[6] His work as financier and as constitutional draughtsman has received all-but-unanimous praise. But there is still no Hamilton legend. Why?

Behind the rounded and remarkable doctrines was a figure almost as paradoxical as Jefferson himself. For the first of the Federalists and the founder of the nation was born a West Indian; the advocate of aristocracy was born not only in poverty abroad but in shame. As a result he said little about his origins. Old John Adams bluntly called him "the bastard son of a Scots peddler"; denigrators of Washington have calculated whether the itinerary of his visit to Barbados with his half-brother Lawrence in 1752 allowed for a diversion to Nevis and have suggested a very straightforward explanation of his fondness in later years for the West Indian adventurer.

[6] *The Shaping of the American Tradition.* N.Y. (1947), I, p. 239.

The facts are clear enough—though they have become so only in recent years—and need no embroidery.

Hamilton was born on 11 Jan. 1755, on the island of Nevis.[7] He was always—perhaps deliberately—vague about the year, and 1757 has long been thought the year of his birth, since he described himself in 1773 as "about sixteen". He was the second son of Rachael Faucitt and James Hamilton. His mother, strikingly beautiful and rumoured to be in part coloured, but in fact of French Huguenot stock, had been married, at the age of sixteen, to a certain John Michael Lavien, a middle-aged merchant of the Danish island of St Croix. There was a son of this marriage: but it was an unhappy affair. The husband won a divorce that, by the stringent law of the time, prevented the wife's re-marriage, and she returned to her native Nevis. There she met James Hamilton, a younger son of an Ayrshire family; he was gentle, scholarly, and unsuccessful; yet he gave to his younger son a family pride that offset the poverty and ignominy of his boyhood. His home in New York was to be named after the family house, "The Grange", in Ayrshire.

The young Hamilton was brought up in Christiansted on St Croix—where his father abandoned his mother, and where, when Alexander was thirteen, his mother died. He worked in Nicholas Cruger's store and showed great talent at business. He never received much affection and

[7] As recent a biographer as Schachner still holds to 1757. So does the American Congress, which declared 1957 to be the Alexander Hamilton Bicentennial Year. But cf. H. Larson, *The American Genealogist*, July 1945 and D. Bobbé, *American Heritage*, vol. VI, No. 4 (June 1955).

grew up gifted, ambitious, and self-contained. He sought success and power in a bigger world, as he wrote in his first extant letter to his friend, Ned Stevens, then at King's College in New York (11 Nov. 1769)—

> ... to confess my weakness, Ned, my ambition is prevalent, so that I contemn the grovelling condition of a clerk or the like, to which my fortune condemns me, and would willingly risk my life, though not my character to exalt my station ... I wish there was a war.

The opportunity came in violent form, more devastating than a war, in the hurricane of August 1772. Hamilton's account of this came to the notice of Hugh Knox, Presbyterian clergyman in the islands, and was published by him in the *Royal Danish-American Gazette*. Knox persuaded the boy to go to Princeton, and provided him with letters of introduction to William Livingston and Elias Boudinot in New Jersey, who became his first— and not his last—mentors; for Hamilton's career, *inter alia*, how far it is possible for a protégé to travel. He appears to have arrived in New Jersey not in 1772, as so many of his biographers hold, but a year later. According to Hercules Mulligan, he first tried to enter Princeton, but made impossible demands on the small staff. At least a year before the Revolution began, Hamilton was a student at King's College, N.Y., absorbing High Toryism from Dr Myles Cooper, but also absorbing—and voicing—revolutionary sentiments in the student clubs and debating societies. The war he sought came and, with it, an enthusiasm for his new country and a determination to shine in her service.

The war provided opportunity; the pamphleteer became a captain in the New York Artillery and, perhaps on Boudinot's, or Nathanael Greene's recommendation, a military secretary to Washington in March 1777. From that point Washington's letters increased in number, in length—and in literary quality. But, like many another clerk in wartime, Hamilton had dreams of military prowess and, with an eye on a political career, perhaps thought them imperative. Passed over in 1781 for the post of Adjutant-General, he quarrelled with Washington and resigned as aide. In July he got his field appointment and saw action at the redoubts at Yorktown.

In December 1780, Hamilton had put the war to that other traditional use of an aide-de-camp; he married General Philip Schuyler's daughter, Elizabeth, and merged his fortunes with those of the rich patronage of the Hudson Valley. He was thought to be twenty-three— he was, in fact, twenty-five—and he had arrived. Already he had drawn up memoranda for Robert Morris on the establishment of a National Bank. After Yorktown he practised as a lawyer, was receiver of continental taxes for New York and represented New York at the Annapolis and Philadelphia conventions. He was appointed Secretary of the Treasury in September 1789, and served until January 1795. The years after Washington's retirement were years of disappointment, of partisanship, and of anticlimax.

The first obstacle, then, to the growth of a reputation was that Hamilton rose from nothing and rose fast. Looking, and believed to be, younger than he was, he was thought of, and described, as precocious and brilliant;

his talents were regarded as mercurial, and the extraordinary capacity he showed for sustained work during the war was appreciated by few except Washington. Surrounded by older men, and flattered by them, his vanity grew. Yet, although no one doubted his patriotism, he was considered an outsider in wartime and was naturally passed over for posts of real responsibility. Adams thought of him in this way to the end, and in 1809 excused his errors on the grounds that he was "not a native of America", and that "he never acquired the feelings and principles of the American people". Hamilton recognised this himself—"Every day proves to me more and more that this American world was not made for me." Moreover, he was backed by men of substance, Boudinot, Schuyler, and Washington; he saw himself as a natural *aristo* and became the advocate and apologist of the Right, a Burke to the great Oaks of the Revolution, but with a skill in finance to match his skill in words. Yet like Burke he was never quite accepted, isolated by his abilities, by his foreignness, and by his arrogance. If in one way he was proof of the accuracy of Dr Johnson's remark that anything can be done with a Scotchman "if he be caught young", he disproved the great panjandrum's other maxim "Slow rises worth by poverty depressed". In the New World careers were open to talent: but even there a man could be too obviously on the make.

The doubts about the man's background and stability were reinforced by his declared beliefs. For Hamilton has earned misdirected and unmerited approval as a designer of the Constitution. He accepted it and worked for it, but only as a second best; and his doubts about its

Portrait of George Washington which hangs in Sulgrave
Manor, the Northamptonshire home of
Washington's ancestors.

Abraham Lincoln.

durability continued until the day he died. He described it in 1802 as "a frail and worthless fabric which I have been endeavouring to prop up". What he admired was discipline and authority in government; what he preached was mercantilism. He subsidised those who invested in manufactures and public securities; he taxed the landed interest. He favoured an "hereditary" chief magistrate, representing the "permanent will" of society and capable of curbing the "turbulent and uncontrouling disposition" of democracy. He wanted an upper house chosen for life on a property basis. "Our real disease", he wrote on the night before he was shot, "is democracy". As a result, a leading student of American conservatism refuses to describe Hamilton as a conservative at all, but as a Federalist who advocated "Rightism run riot".

> If he was conservative in practical politics and in his concern for property, he was reactionary in his devotion to monarchy and hereditary aristocracy, visionary in his scheme for an industrial America, and who-knows-what —radical, reactionary, or just plain opportunistic?—in his eagerness to reduce the states to an inferior position. His basic ideas, which he voiced on the floor of the Convention, were irrelevant in the American environment and were certainly not those of a man who knew and cherished the American tradition. ... No man could be so indifferent to the established order, full of schemes for its alteration, dazzled by plutocracy, and casual about centralized power and still lay claim to the title of conservative.[8]

This formidable indictment reflects Hamilton's past.

[8] Clinton Rossiter, "The Giants of American Conservatism", *American Heritage*, vol. VI, No. 6 (Oct. 1955).

A.P.—E

His economic-cum-political views were shaped in fact less by America than by his youth in the store in the lush sugar islands, where prosperity depended—hurricanes permitting—on an elaborate trading system, and where society was hierarchical. He had no sympathy with Jefferson's farmer-democrats, but at least the rich, the well-born and the able were given every encouragement, and the fluidity of a free society allowed them to be creative, not destructive.

But in the last analysis it was neither Hamilton's background nor his ideas that lost him sympathy. No society has been more sympathetic than the American to the immigrant and the man on the make, as the Revolutionary catalogue and later years attest. Ideas about the Constitution varied widely; Paine and Jefferson and George Mason had their own doubts about it, of a different kind from Hamilton's. Hamilton's failure was a failure of personality; the creed was bigger than the man. Although his financial doctrines were wise, he could be as inconsistent as Jefferson himself. In *The Federalist* (Nos. 12 and 21) he declared that "the genius of the people" hated excises: but they were an essential part of his revenue system in 1791; and in 1794 he was employing force to crush the resistance to them of the Whisky Rebels in Pennsylvania. The advocate of isolation in *The Federalist* (No. 11) became in 1794 the notorious Anglophile of the Jay Treaty; the supporter of free elections and free choice in 1787 tried in 1800 to nullify the popular vote and threatened force in the process. He claimed in 1787, and in 1791–4, to "think continentally"; yet by 1800 he was the not-fully-avowed leader of the High Federalists, at odds with President Adams and wrecking both Adams' administration and his own party. Increasingly he advocated the use of armies: in 1794 to crush Pennsylvanian farmers; in 1798, when he became Inspector-General, to go to war with France— or perhaps to embark on a great crusade as Libertador in Spanish America; in 1800 to preserve Federalist power in New York. "In times like these", he told John Jay, "it will not do to be over-scrupulous". He split with Adams because the President kept peace with France. He thought Jefferson ought to go to war to gain Louisiana: but, when Jefferson achieved its purchase in a staggering diplomatic triumph, Hamilton wrote

> the advantage of the acquisition appears too distant and remote to strike the mind of a sober politician with much force. . . . It . . . must hasten the dismemberment of a large portion of our country, or a dissolution of the Government.[9]

The passionate nationalist could become the most bitter and irrational of partisans.

To these contradictions he added a capacity for quarrelling with almost every one of his closest associates. The high integrity and devotion to his country were outmatched by a devotion to his own career that involved him in endless intrigues. He quarrelled with Washington in 1781, when his Commander-in-Chief charged him with tardiness and disrespect. "I replied, without petulancy, but with decision; 'I am not conscious of it, sir, but since you have thought it necessary to tell me so, we part'." He explained to his father-in-law that he

[9] *New York Evening Post*, Tuesday, 5 Jul. 1803.

"always disliked the office of an aide-de-camp as having in it a kind of personal dependence". Washington, he said, was "neither remarkable for delicacy nor good temper". Yet Washington sought to apologise within the hour, to be sharply rebuffed, and he continued, in 1781, as in 1789, to harbour no grudge. Though both men were under strain—it was eight months before Yorktown—the fact remains that the older man emerges with the greater honour.

Washington was fully aware of Hamilton's ambition, but appreciated his talents. Adams was less kind and, like his party, suffered acutely at his hands after 1796. His Cabinet was staffed with Hamilton's men; and for four years Hamilton was "the worm at the root of the peach", "the Creole adventurer", "the Creole bastard". Adams' son, John Quincy, thought Hamilton's ambition

> transcendent, and his disposition to intrigue irrepressible ... he was of that class of characters which cannot bear a rival—haughty, overpowering, jealous, bitter and violent in his personal enmities, and little scrupulous of the means he used against those who stood in the way of his ambition.[10]

If the Adamses cannot be thought impartial, Noah Webster, a staunch Federalist, equally deplored Hamilton's wrecking of the party. In his *Open Letter to General Hamilton*, in 1800, he said "your ambition, pride and overbearing temper have destined you to be the evil

[10] John Quincy Adams' MSS. "Parties in the United States" in *The Selected Writings of John and John Quincy Adams*, eds. Koch and Peden. N.Y. (1946), pp. 329-30.

genius of this country". Abigail Adams saw the trend even more sharply. "That man," she said, "would become a second Bonaparty if he was possessed of equal power!" The charge was valid; Hamilton's hero was Julius Caesar.

The years after 1800 were years of failure. Although devoted to his wife, he was not faithful, and was ready to reveal his liaison with Maria Reynolds rather than allow the blackmailing activities of her husband to be thought attributable to any political immorality. With the Republican victory in 1800, largely due to his own quarrel with Adams, his power had gone. By ensuring Jefferson's election as President he made a mortal enemy of Aaron Burr, who had tied with Jefferson in the Electoral College.

In 1801 Philip, Hamilton's oldest son, was shot in a duel and his daughter, Angelica, became permanently insane with grief; his wife was pregnant with her eighth child at the time. He emerged from his private life in 1804 to oppose Burr's bid for the Governorship of New York, which carried with it the danger of a secession of New York and New England from the Union. The charges ran high; and for some of them, of which he heard at second hand, Burr demanded satisfaction. Trumbull always argued that Hamilton need not have fought and it is not clear from his letters to Burr that Hamilton meant to accept his challenge. He seems in these last years to have been changing and to have been facing religious and ethical problems for the first time. He recognised that some of his criticisms of Burr had been "extremely severe", and that, according to the code of honour, he

owed Burr the right to shoot at him at twelve paces. He
made his plans quietly.

On Tuesday night, 10 Jul. 1804, as one account has it
—even here there are variants—he arranged for his
twelve-year-old son, John Church, to sleep with him.
The son never forgot how he and his father recited the
Lord's Prayer in unison. Before dawn on Wednesday
he rose without waking the boy, rode the eight miles
from "The Grange" to New York City and was rowed
across the Hudson to the New Jersey Heights of
Weehawken.

> It was shortly after seven when the two duellists
> stood to their stations in the wooded clearing high above
> the river. At the word "Present" two reports rang out,
> one shortly behind the other; and the shorter of the
> antagonists, rising convulsively on tiptoe, staggered a
> little to the left and fell headlong upon his face. As the
> surgeon hastily examined the gaping hole in his right
> side, the wounded man had just strength to gasp before
> fainting, "This is a mortal wound, Doctor . . ."
>
> And fast as a spreading bush fire, the news went
> through New York City that Colonel Burr had shot
> General Hamilton in a duel—that Hamilton was dying—
> was already lying dead in Mr. Bayard's house at Green-
> wich.[11]

The bullet had pierced his liver and lodged in his spine.
He lingered on in great pain and died the following
afternoon.

Hamilton was a man of great gifts, great achievements

[11] William Coleman, *A Collection of the Facts and Documents relative
to the Death of Major-General Alexander Hamilton* (N.Y. 1804),
pp. 19-20.

and transcendent integrity, perhaps the most creative figure thrown up by the American Revolution. Like some other eminent conservative leaders, he was a social climber, and he cultivated men with power. He had no sympathy for the West, or for notions of local self-government, or for the rights of the States. Although his view of the Union was synoptic, it hardly included its citizens; administration was more important than the ends it served. Like his hero, Caesar, he was obsessed by the love of fame—"the ruling passion of the noblest minds", he called it himself. As Adams noted, he was too fond of crises and too ready to use armies to be a good democrat; and he did not hide his scorn for "the people". For a democracy his very talents could carry their own danger; love of power and lack of compassion could be as serious a menace to the republican experiment as conspiracy within and without. The death of Hamilton at the hands of Burr ended a double threat to the future of the state.

LINCOLN BEFORE HIS ELECTION[1]

The United States is quite as addicted to holy days as
Catholic Europe or the Islamic world, and among them
three are pre-eminent: 4 July, the day on which, it is
believed (inaccurately as it happens), the Founding
Fathers signed the Declaration of Independence; 22
February, Washington's birthday; and 12 February, the
birthday of Abraham Lincoln. Of these the last has come
to hold a special place in the calendar, as Lincoln has
come to hold a special, perhaps the central, place in
American hagiology.

The reasons are many. One, the rags to riches theme,
from log cabin to White House; born to an illiterate and
wandering frontiersman and with hardly any formal
schooling, a failure at forty, he was at fifty the President
of the United States at the most critical moment in its
history. Two, the transition from awkward and hesitant
Westerner, ill-versed in Eastern politeness and in person
ugly and ungainly, to skilful and dexterous politician, the
symbol of success in war and the leader of a reunited
country. Three, the President in the midst of war who
yet stayed civilian-minded, who, even when he studied
military manuals to prepare himself for active command,
remained the humanitarian, prompt to pardon offenders,

[1] [Originally published in *History Today*, x (1960), pp. 737-46.]

forgiving towards deserters and gentle towards the
bereaved; the war leader and elect of the nation had
never found it easy even to discipline his own children.
Four, the Liberator, plagued by the slavery question,
who was able to emancipate the slaves from January 1863,
and to whom the war then became a campaign to safe-
guard a covenant. And fifth, beyond and including all
these, the folksy man himself, with his tall tales and rough
humour, the brooding figure addicted to melancholy and
acquainted with grief; the human figure, bothered by a
shrewish and complaining wife, who in his high office
was untouched by pride or pomp, to whom assassination
in the hour of his triumph brought the final apotheosis of
martyrdom. He was shot on a Good Friday, sacrificed,
it seemed, for the redemption of the Union he loved.
"Now he belongs to the ages", said Stanton—rarely in
life an admirer. And the ages have seized on his story to
make it the most significant personal saga in American
history, and to see in Lincoln the stereotype not only of
the democratic opportunities offered by the New World
but also of its conscience and humanity. In the Lincoln
story it has been hard to avoid the use of the term
Saviour.

> Lincoln, six feet one in his stocking feet,
> The lank man, knotty and tough as a hickory rail,
> Whose hands were always too big for white-kid gloves,
> Whose wit was a coonskin sack of dry, tall tales,
> Whose weathered face was homely as a plowed
>   field— . . .
> Honesty rare as a man without self-pity,
> Kindness as large and plain as a prairie-wind,
> And a self-confidence like an iron bar.

Or as the school-children of Illinois honour him each
12 February, turning towards Springfield as if to a Mecca
as they chant—

> A blend of mirth and sadness,
> Smiles and tears,
> A quaint Knight-errant of the pioneers,
> A homely hero born a star in sod,
> A peasant prince, a masterpiece of God.

Historical research is usually prompt to destroy
mythology—even if few among contemporary American
historians aspire, these days, to be called "debunkers".
The Lincoln legend has, however, proved to be well
founded. It is impossible not to admire his personal
qualities—his modesty, humour, patience, and compassion—his uncanny skill as a war-leader through the
agony of a civil war, or his faith in the Union. The
legends that have been destroyed by recent research are
mainly those assiduously fostered by William Herndon,
Lincoln's law partner—in particular the tale of Lincoln's
jilting of Mary Todd at the church door, and how she
later married him for spite. It cannot be claimed that it
was a happy marriage, but the reason now seems clearly
to have been Mrs Lincoln's mental instability, which
increased in the war years. About the greatness of the
man himself, after the war began, there has been little
controversy. Queries do remain, however, about his role
in the years before Beauregard's guns opened up on
Sumter. Moreover, the legend has itself contrived to
minimise some striking features of his early life; it has
certainly obscured the extent both of his political
ambition and of his political dexterity; and it has in

particular obscured his long hesitations on the slavery
question. He who earned the title of "the great Emancipa-
tor" came to emancipation very late, and with marked
reluctance.

In the family migration from Kentucky to Indiana and
finally to Illinois, Lincoln had been a jack-of-all-trades—
farm-labourer, rail splitter, flat-boatman on the Missis-
sippi, storekeeper, postmaster, assistant surveyor of roads.
He held no job for long, but he came to know people and
to be known by them. He was phenomenally strong and
striking, however ungainly—well over six feet in height,
a wrestler, a captain in the Black Hawk War, and a good
teller of tales, many of them robust. Not until his
election for Sangamon County to the Illinois State
Legislature (at the second attempt) in 1834, did he begin
the study of law. And as his later law partner William
Herndon tells us, he rarely spent long reading law books.
The fact was that from the first, despite the poor schooling, the droll manners, and the lack of grace, he had
political ambitions.

Not only ambitions but skill, and some success. His
prominence in state politics—he served four terms in the
state legislature—derived largely from the fact that he
helped to have the state capital moved to the county seat,
Springfield. This was politics—then as now—that his
county could appreciate; it mattered more than policies
or principles.

Where principles were concerned, what was striking
about Lincoln in Illinois politics in the 1830s—the
heyday of Jacksonian Democracy—was that he was,
after all, not a Democrat but a Whig. Raised on the

frontier, he was yet no agrarian. He cast his first vote in 1832 for Henry Clay; he preferred "the American system"—the programme of internal improvements, stable currency, and high tariffs—to the programme of equality and reform; he held the Jacksonians to be traitors to Jefferson's ideals. The poor boy was in the rich man's party; he was ultimately to marry into it; and his wife, a Todd from the Lexington Bluegrass, was never to allow him to forget the social gulf between them. In all the discussions of Lincoln as a product of American democracy, a noticeable feature is his determination to rise by his own boot-straps and to become not only successful, but dignified. He was embarrassed in 1860 by the propaganda about his origins, and by the rail-splitter image. Prone to tell a folksy tale, he did not really welcome replies in kind. As Seward was to learn, he could keep his own counsel. "He was not a social man", says Herndon—"too reflective, too abstracted"—"a reticent, secretive, shut-mouth man". Behind the rough exterior he was never a Jacksonian. Despite the Turner thesis, the frontier has in fact produced as many natural aristocrats as it has produced conformists.

Lincoln's single term in the national congress (1847–9), generally undistinguished, had about it again many of the characteristics of the cautious politician. He was Illinois' only Whig representative, having defeated a formidable backwoods preacher, Peter Cartwright. In his campaign, Lincoln had not opposed the Mexican War, but when his party denounced the war as both Democratic and unjust, Lincoln strongly supported their charges. In the course of doing so he asserted the right of any people, or of a "majority of any portion of such people", to "shake off the existing government, and form a new one"—a viewpoint impossible to reconcile with his stand in 1861. His criticism of the Mexican War and his loyalty to his party lost him the support of his state: he was to many a "second Benedict Arnold", speaking for the East, where the war was unpopular, and disregarding the West, where it was popular. Although his party won the 1848 election, they did not carry his district. Lincoln resumed his law practice—"I was losing interest in politics", he wrote later.

The lack of interest remained until the passing of the Kansas–Nebraska Act in 1854, and the repeal of the Missouri Compromise that it carried with it. This, the work of Senator Stephen Douglas of Illinois, made it possible for the settlers in Kansas and Nebraska, before being granted statehood, to vote for the introduction of slavery. It re-opened the slavery controversy, and brought Lincoln back into politics.

The slavery issue was not only the most perplexing of American—and human—issues. It posed particular problems to the Middle Western states, as it did to the territories, at a time when American society, already very mobile, was becoming polyglot. In the decade 1850–60 the population of Illinois doubled (from 851,470 to 1,711,951) and its foreign-born population trebled (by 1860 it was over 300,000). Nativism was already a feature of the Eastern states—quite as marked a feature, oddly, as the moral concern over the wickedness of slavery—and a dangerously popular Know-Nothing party developed. For this Lincoln had no sympathy.

I am not a Know-nothing. How could I be? How can anyone who abhors the oppression of Negroes be in favor of degrading classes of white people? Our progress in degeneracy appears to me to be pretty rapid. As a nation we began by declaring that "all men are created equal." We now practically read it "all men are created equal except negroes." When the Know-nothings get control, it will read "all men are created equal, except negroes and foreigners and Catholics." When it comes to this, I shall prefer emigrating to some country where they make no pretense of loving liberty,—to Russia, for instance, where despotism can be taken pure, and without the base alloy of Hypocracy [*sic*].

But slavery was a much less straightforward matter. Always compassionate and tolerant, Lincoln detested the institution of slavery; equally he deplored the campaigns of the abolitionists who fought slavery by extra-constitutional means, just as he deplored the riots of those who sought to deprive the abolitionists of the right to speak their minds. It was at Alton, Illinois, that Elijah Lovejoy had been murdered. The abolitionists, especially their leader in the West, Theodore Dwight Weld, were far more a problem in the 1840s and 1850s than the pro-slavery advocates—Weld indeed a more important figure, it now seems, than Garrison.

And Lincoln faithfully reflected in these years the viewpoint of his section. The tale that on his second visit to New Orleans, when he was just twenty-one, he saw a mulatto girl being sold on the block, and that "the iron entered his soul", causing him to vow to "hit slavery hard"—this is now suspect among Lincoln scholars. In fact, during his formative years he appears not to have been particularly concerned about slavery. He lived in an area where slaves were rare; his family hailed from Virginia, and if this did not make him pro-Southern at least he seems to have shared the contemporary Southern belief that slavery would gradually disappear. He did nothing when in the state legislature to interfere with the severe laws that were in force against free Negroes or runaway slaves; he did not denounce—as so many did—the Fugitive Slave Law, despite the obvious hardships to free Negroes—"I confess I hate to see the poor creatures hunted down . . . but I bite my lips and keep quiet". When the Illinois legislature denounced abolitionists, and came down on the pro-slavery side, Lincoln refused, it is true, to support the majority: but he afterwards justified his position by the unexceptionable statement that "the institution of slavery is founded on injustice and bad policy but . . . the promulgation of abolition doctrines tends to increase rather than abate its evils". As a good lawyer Lincoln respected the Constitution; slavery where it existed must be left alone, and allowed to die a natural death—if it would. It is not surprising but often forgotten that such moderation, at a time when tempers ran high, brought him no distinction—and some obloquy. To Wendell Phillips he was "that slavehound from Illinois". However inaccurate this was, Lincoln was certainly no crusader.

When Douglas brought forward his proposals to open new territory to slavery, he split the Democratic Party and lost the support of much Northern opinion. It was thought—probably unfairly—that he was seeking to win Southern support for his own Presidential ambitions;

it was thought—with more justification—that he was
planning a railway route through the Kansas–Nebraska
territory; it is certain that he was not excited about
slavery, and that he was misled by his own certainty that
neither Kansas nor Nebraska would be suited to a slave
economy anyway. As he put it in the Lincoln–Douglas
debates, "I care more for the great principle of self-
government, the right of the people to rule, than I do for
all the Negroes in Christendom".

Superficially, Douglas was right, as his triumph over
Lincoln in the Senatorial contest in 1858 revealed: but
Lincoln's political flair here proved deeper and shrewder
than Douglas's. Between 1854 and 1856 Lincoln moved
from the Whig to the newly-founded Republican Party.
He did so cautiously; in 1855 he sought unsuccessfully
the Whig nomination for the Senate. Although the new
party was built on a series of often quite contradictory
programmes and issues—the tariff, internal improvements, prohibitionism—Lincoln steered clear of all of
these in Illinois. When Douglas was making it plain that
he was not pro-slavery, but was ready to permit slavery
in the territories, Lincoln was making it equally plain that
he was not an abolitionist, but that he was opposed to
slavery in the territories. Douglas's stand could only win
support in the South, and on the Southern border—and
tepid support at that. Lincoln's could win approval
everywhere outside the South. And in his opposition to
the extension of slavery to the territories, Lincoln was
always firm and consistent. A thread of certainty was
appearing; and a strong thread it was, for it was Lincoln's
refusal to sunder it that caused the Civil War.

He was slow to condemn slavery as such. He did so now and then, but never formally until 1854, and always accompanying his condemnations by a frank avowal that he did not know what to do about it—"if all earthly power were given me, I should not know what to do as to the existing institution". There was, then, distaste for the institution, a firm front against its further extension and a frank avowal of uncertainty how to curb it without offending the South—or the law of the land. But there was something more than this, greatly appealing to Illinois, and that was the theme that the Western states, like the territories, were for white men—free men but white men. Alongside every sentence in every speech condemning the wickedness of slavery and stressing the superior merits of a free to a slave society, there is the equal emphasis that the Negro must not be given political or social equality. The Negro was the equal of the white: but he must not be given citizenship. The Republican Party in the North-west inherited both free-soil sentiments and, in some degree, nativism; if not as cold-blooded about slavery as Douglas, it did not want Negroes, free or slave, in its borders. Its theme-song in Missouri, as advocated by Frank Blair on the masthead of his *Daily Missouri Democrat*, was "White Men for Missouri and Missouri for White Men".

Lincoln's greatest achievement as a politician before the election of 1860—his skills did not stop then—lay in the dexterity with which he used this issue, bred by the section in which he was raised, to reconcile many conflicting groups and win them over to his side. It was not that Lincoln took a moral line, although he sometimes

A.P.—F

did so—and this was noted in New England, where moral lines were more traditional, and easier, than elsewhere. Hence he was noted with favour "back East". It was not that Lincoln supported abolitionism—he did not, although many abolitionists noted with favour only his condemnations of "the peculiar institution". Nor was it that he opposed the extension of slavery to the territories out of a mere trust in political compromise itself— as Clay had done in 1850. He had found an issue that touched all these and transcended them, and won him fame in the North-west. He expressed it in his speech at Peoria in 1854 when he spoke of the future of the territories:

> We want them for homes of free white people. This they cannot be, to any considerable extent, if slavery shall be planted within them. Slave States are places for poor white people to remove from, not to remove to. New free States are the places for poor people to go to, and better their condition. For this use the nation needs these Territories.

The argument—he used it repeatedly in the next six years—was an argument not for equality—of black and white—but for freedom—for whites. It was the fear of poorer whites, almost all of them immigrants into the West and many of them of foreign origin, that they might now have to compete in hitherto-free states with the labour of slaves, that brought them, in the North-west, into the Republican Party. It was not difficult for the Republican Party to build around this theme those other planks—free homesteads, a railway to the Pacific, a protective tariff—that were in the end to make of it the party of progress, expansion, and the full dinner pail. The pioneer of the 1850s was, after all, often the father of the entrepreneur of the 1890s. If Lincoln's father was an illiterate nomad, Lincoln's son was Ambassador to the Court of St James and President of the Pullman Car Company. The generation that lived in the sod-house—like that which fought the Indian—was very short; but if short in actual span of years it too has been long in legends.

It was easy for Douglas, in the debate of 1858, to point to the flaws in Lincoln's case—to accuse him of being, in his "house-divided" speech, a sectional leader only, whose viewpoint assumed "a war of section"; to task him with favouring equality for Negroes; and to make the charge that he adapted his speeches to suit the varied attitudes of the state. He was, said Douglas, "jet black" in the North, "a decent mulatto" in the centre and "almost white" in the South. And the charge was true: in Chicago it was "all men are created equal"; in the South "the superior position must go to the white race". Lincoln was still a moderate—opposed to abolition, opposed to the repeal of the Fugitive Slave Laws, opposed to Negro citizenship and to social and political equality of white and black. The free Negro, H. Ford Douglass, thought his programme no better than that of Stephen Douglas. But in all his dexterity, Lincoln never abandoned the central argument: that slavery must not be permitted to expand. If the Dred Scott decision of the Supreme Court in 1857 were permitted to stand—that slavery could not be excluded from the territories—where could slavery be halted? "Popular sovereignty" could not be reconciled with the Dred Scott decision. The Democratic

Party had become a "conspiracy . . . for the sole purpose of nationalising slavery". Douglas, in the debates, was the realist, and was right to think that it was idle to thrash out an issue that geography itself would settle. Douglas won the election—since Senators were then chosen by the legislature, and there the apportionment of seats gave the Democrats control. But Lincoln won more popular votes than Douglas, and it was clear now to the nation, as to Illinois, that he saw further and touched deeper chords.

The 1858 debates gave Lincoln a national platform. The compromise programme of Illinois that brought some satisfaction to all the groups in the variegated Republican Party—but not complete satisfaction to any —became the platform of 1860. In the "house divided" references, Lincoln had touched on the moral issue, although he was careful not to develop it too far. He touched it again in the debates with Douglas at Galesburg and at Quincy—slavery was "a moral, social, and political wrong". But it was still *festina lente*. And Lincoln sought the Presidential nomination in 1860 as he had sought previous success—by speeches and correspondence emphasising moderation, by managing party business, by being active and being seen to be active. Herndon was right to say "He was always calculating and planning ahead. His ambition was a little engine that knew no rest." Throughout 1859 he campaigned, as the leading Western Republican, in Ohio and Indiana, Iowa and Wisconsin. When he delivered the Cooper Institute speech in New York in February 1860—the speech and the photograph that in retrospect he thought gave him the Republican nomination—he held to the same note: denial of abolitionism; distaste for John Brown's radicalism; sympathy for the South—but no support for any proposed extension of slavery to the territories of the United States. This was for Lincoln the central precept, ordained by the Founding Fathers.

When he was nominated as the choice of Illinois Republicans at the Republican Convention in 1860—a convention that met, helpfully, in the "Wigwam" in Chicago (a lumber shack built to hold 10,000 and which 40,000 sought to enter)—his efforts were crowned with success. The Democrats had already held their Convention, in Charleston, S.C., and had broken up in disorder. The Southerners wanted positive protection for slaveholding and nominated Breckinridge of Kentucky. The "regular" Democrats nominated Douglas. There were likely to be at least two Democratic Parties; there might be more. Whoever won the Republican nomination was therefore almost certain of victory. This put a premium on moderation, especially if the key states —Illinois, Indiana, Pennsylvania—were to be won. Seward of New York was too biting and too radical, and the redoubtable editor of the *New York Tribune*, Horace Greeley, opposed him. This seemed no time for talk of "the irrepressible conflict" and "the higher law". Chase of Ohio could not control his own state; he was precise, aloof, and abstemious.

Even so, the nomination of Lincoln—like his whole career—demanded skilful mechanics. There is a considerable and rival literature on the question of the division of credit for the dexterities of the "Wigwam" between O. H. Browning, Joseph Medill, and Charles Ray of the *Chicago Tribune*, and Jesse Fell (great-grandfather of Adlai Stevenson). Probably the credit should really go to his campaign manager, stout Judge David Davis, an old friend of the Illinois circuit, with his headquarters in the Tremont House. One of Davis's happiest devices was to print and issue bogus tickets for Lincoln supporters, who, there ahead of time, got into the Convention—and kept Seward's men out. Another was to place stentor-voiced supporters at key points—one of them was reputed to be able to shout across Lake Michigan. And with effect, for when Lincoln was nominated, one witness said that "A thousand steam whistles, ten acres of hotel gongs, a tribe of Comanches, headed by a choice vanguard from pandemonium might have mingled in the scene unnoticed."

Lincoln had instructed Davis to make no bargains. This was honoured as scrupulously as such adages normally are—and are expected to be. "Lincoln ain't here", said Davis, "and don't know what we have to meet so we will go ahead as if we hadn't heard from him, and he must ratify it." The promises were made, and Lincoln's later Cabinet revealed the extent of them. "They have gambled me all round, bought and sold me a hundred times." But this too is normal; and it is normal in democratic politics genuinely to deplore the means even as one esteems the end.

With 465 delegates present and 233 votes necessary for victory, on the first ballot Seward had $173\frac{1}{2}$, Lincoln 102, Cameron of Pennsylvania $50\frac{1}{2}$, Chase 49, Bates 48, and the remainder scattered. On the second ballot, Cameron's name was withdrawn to Lincoln's advantage (Cameron was to become his Secretary of War): Seward had 184½, Lincoln 181, Chase 42½, Bates 45. When, on the third ballot, 4 Ohio voters transferred to Lincoln, a landslide followed.

In the ensuing months, the landslide spread through the continent. As the South talked of secession—not original talk, it is true, in South or North—if the "Black Republican" were elected, Lincoln sat in Springfield. He made very few speeches, although he talked a great deal to political leaders and delegations. He did little, however, to placate the South. And on 6 Nov. 1860, he was chosen President by a large electoral majority (Lincoln 180, Breckinridge of Kentucky 72, Bell 39, Douglas 12)— but with only 40 per cent of the popular vote (Lincoln 1,866,452; Douglas 1,376,957; Breckinridge 849,781; Bell 588,879). In ten Southern states not a single popular vote was cast for him; he failed to carry his own county in Illinois. But he carried every free state in the North except New Jersey. Moderation paid; the White House awaited him. His silence did not; South Carolina seceded from the Union.

Through the anxious four months between election and inauguration, the silence continued. And Buchanan, the retiring President, took no action. While state after state withdrew, and a Southern Confederacy was formed, Lincoln made his plans in Springfield, but made no statements of policy. He would move, as always, slowly. For what was now emerging was the second theme; as the President-elect, he had an oath to keep, requiring the perpetuation of the Union, for the Union was perpetual.

This to Lincoln as lawyer, politician, and citizen was now the first priority. Nothing must be done by him—or by any man or combination of men—that would risk the break-up of the Union. "If I could save the Union by emancipating all the slaves I would do so; if I could save it by emancipating none I would do it; if I could save it by emancipating some and not others, I would do that too." This carried with it respect for the Constitution and the rights guaranteed by it—including slavery where it existed. As late as 1861 he was ready to amend the Constitution to guarantee slavery in the states, and generals who announced emancipation in their commands were promptly rebuked.

Equally, he had won his election on a political platform that for him was quite as binding as his Presidential oath. His refusal to consider the territorial extension of slavery wrecked the Crittenden compromise proposals. "Stand firm", he told Hyman Trumbull. "The tug has to come, and better now than at any time hereafter." "Hold firm", he told Elihu Washburne, "as with a chain of steel". The consistent thread was now visible through all the stress and pressures put on him.

Lincoln was without training in executive office, and not, thus far, quick in action. Advice and requests poured in, of all kinds—from wives seeking promotion for their husbands; from Southern belles ("For God sake Dear Sir give us women some assurance that you will protect us, for we are the greatest Slaves in the South"); from supporters seeking "a little of the needful"; from Pinkerton, the detective, enclosing a private cipher code (in which apparently the code-word for the Secretary of

War was "pea-nuts" and for the President himself plain "nuts"); from enemies telling him to give up—or to shoot himself.

Lincoln left Springfield for Washington on 11 Feb. 1861. Because of reports of likely attempts at assassination he entered the city secretly, at night. His speeches *en route* had done nothing to placate the South. General Winfield Scott had been ordered to be ready to "hold or retake" the forts in the South as circumstances might require. But the Inaugural Address was conciliatory. Lincoln once again disclaimed any intention of interfering with slavery in the states; all Federal laws must be observed—including the laws compelling the return of fugitive slaves; the Union, however, must and would be preserved. But there was no way in which the oath to maintain the Constitution and preserve the Union could be squared with Secession. "In your hands, my dissatisfied fellow-countrymen, and not in mine, is the momentous issue of civil war. You have no oath registered in heaven to destroy the Government; while I shall have the most solemn one to 'preserve, protect and defend' it."

Lincoln won his election not by moral greatness, or by compassion for white or black, but by political skills of a high order. He was to reveal greatness in the years ahead, moral as well as political. Earnest he was, with remarkable insight into the essence of the controversy; and firm he was to show himself. But little of this was evident in 1860, least of all to his Cabinet. The ill-dressed and awkward figure, with a high nasal inflexion in his voice, was—to Seward as to the country—an unknown quantity, even perhaps a "Simple Susan". He had shown uncanny skill in compromising on many questions. He had also shown that there were for him some issues on which there could be no compromise, and no surrender. "Hard as a rock and soft as drifting fog" is Sandburg's phrase.

The issues raised by Fort Sumter, an undermanned Federal fort commanding the narrows leading to Charleston harbour and held by Federal troops, whose supplies were running short, were his first test as President—the first of many. But that is another story.

WOODROW WILSON AND THE
FIRST WORLD WAR[1]

One of the most curious phenomena in the writing of
recent American history is the failure of American
historians to agree on a verdict on Woodrow Wilson.
This is the more surprising since for two decades now
American Presidents have been, in their varied and at
times conflicting ways, world leaders. Isolationism is no
longer fashionable, nor indeed tenable; those who in the
past might have been its foremost advocates have
recently been found on the Far Right, supporters of
McCarthy, MacArthur, or of brinkmanship in varied
forms. Historians, prompt to reflect the preoccupations
of their own times—one has to understand the present, it
is now fashionable to say, in order to understand the past
—have in any event long been doubting the accuracy of
isolationism as a description of American foreign policy.
Honoured when it suited her purposes, and binding as
myth, it was ignored in 1798 and again in 1812; even its
bible, the Monroe Doctrine of 1823, was accompanied by
expressions of sympathy for struggling Greece; it was
never honoured except in piety in the Caribbean, in
Latin America or in the Pacific; and since 1898 it has
been essentially discarded as a Great Rule. Alexander

[1] [Originally published in two parts in *History Today*, x (1960),
pp. 149-57 and pp. 223-31.]

DeConde, in his *Entangling Alliance*, has recently doubted whether the much-cited Washington or Jefferson texts were designed to be binding on posterity, and has suggested realistically that they were, like most state papers, meant for the day they were issued.

Yet, sympathetic though the climate has become to idealism, and even to interventionism in foreign affairs, to liberal causes and crusading leaders, there has been no concerted effort to resurrect and worship Wilson as America's greatest international crusader. There has been little emotional appeal about the picture of the stricken warrior in his bath chair, watching after 1919 the wrecking of his efforts that spelt doom for his party and for the League of Nations, and thus made likely a second World War. When, from time to time, appeals have been made to him in these terms, they have been made by politicians rather than by historians. His own contemporary biographer, Ray Stannard Baker, did, of course, see him as hero. Something of this kind was attempted for a short period in 1941 and 1942, notably by Paul Birdsall in his *Versailles, Twenty Years After*, and the centenary of his birth produced many tributes, particularly an admirable assessment in *The Virginia Quarterly Review* (Autumn 1956). But, even then, no major claims for him were made. Nor are they being made as yet by Professor Arthur Link, in his detailed biography, of which five volumes have thus far appeared. It is to be matched by a forty-volume edition of his *Papers* but—thus far at least—his study does not portray a Presidential leader cast in the Lincoln or even in the Washington mould. Why is there no Wilson legend?

I

We are suffering here from hindsight, of course, if we
assume that Wilson in 1912 was, in any major degree,
concerned with foreign policy. He was not. A student
and teacher of American constitutional history, his pre-
occupation was with the operation of government; and,
as President, he expected to have to deal mainly with
domestic problems. He had shown his skill as a party
leader in New Jersey—at least, during his first few
months in office—in putting through a considerable
programme of reform. His interest lay, apparently, in
municipal government and education, in food and factory
inspection, workmen's compensation, hours, and conditions of labour. This suggests that he was in the
broadest sense a Progressive: but, in fact, he was a
laissez-faire Liberal—"The history of liberty", he said,
"is the history of the limitation of the governmental
power". There is little evidence of a passionate interest
in Progressivism as a creed before his decision to run for
Governor. His speeches as President of Princeton were
mainly on educational themes—and able and constructive
speeches they were. Although it is often said that Wilson
was in the situation of Pitt the Younger, a domestic
reformer plagued after 1914 by questions of foreign
policy, there is equally small evidence for this. As Harley
Notter has shown, in his *The Origins of the Foreign Policy
of Woodrow Wilson*, all the essentials of Wilson's thought
on foreign policy had been formulated before he became
President: the faith in constitutionalism, the dislike of
Big Business in its operations at home and abroad, the

belief that the United States could be a force for order and for morality in world affairs. But as yet these as principles were implicit, not to say vague, part of the common political jargon of the day; and they were to be sorely tested. So, too, was the man's character.

Long before he became President, Wilson had campaigned for leadership, for authority and responsibility in government, against the anonymity of Congressional power. "Somebody must be trusted." The emphasis on personal authority was reflected in an authoritativeness of manner—an authoritativeness that hid flaws and dangers. The high-mindedness carried with it from the first a good conceit of itself; and it could repel. Raymond Robins, the Chicago Progressive who was later active in Russia, left the Democratic Party in 1912 after a luncheon with Wilson, because he got the impression that Wilson felt "I'm a tremendous person and you don't seem to appreciate it yet." The fact was that Wilson came to politics too late—he was nearly fifty-four when he was elected Governor of New Jersey—and he had not been a "mixer" as an academic. He had many of the characteristics of the South—a strong sense of honour and an unbending expectation that others would live by the same code as himself, a prickly integrity, devotion to good causes, and the luxury—more satisfying to himself than others—of plain speaking. With these characteristics he shared others also rooted in the planter's code: a quest in politics for victory rather than for agreement, a certain condescension in his personal attitudes, indeed a strongly personal view of politics as less a matter of ideals and causes than of triumph or disaster for himself.

"A very virtuous man, and an obstinate one too", said Spring-Rice. House told a British friend that the only way to handle Wilson was: "Never begin by arguing; discover a common hate, exploit it, get the President warmed up and then start on your business." Integrity, as so often, was wrapped up with egotism; there was little charity for his friends, as House and Tumulty were to discover, and none for his enemies; his faith in himself was rooted in a Scotch-Irish Presbyterian background, a Calvinist acceptance of order (and of segregation) in society, a certain patrician quality that was as much self-induced as native to the South. For the force that drove Wilson was nervous as well as inherited; he was never physically strong; aloof and shy, he needed reassurance and love—and found that they came more readily from women than men; the successful reformer who yet remained cold and lonely, he was from the first curiously vulnerable.

Nor were the qualities strictly intellectual. There were important gaps in Wilson's education: little knowledge of science, of art and music, or of languages. He confessed that, after becoming President of Princeton, he had no time for serious reading. His years from 1902 to 1910 were indeed political rather than intellectual: he saw himself as engaged in a "fight" with Dean West and with the Princeton clubs; and the campaign for Governor hid the fact of academic escape and defeat. At Princeton there were clear educational issues at stake, and on them Wilson lost. He acted inconsistently and without finesse, and took defeat badly. Princeton asked for his resignation before the result of the election was known. And in 1910

Wilson was completely devoid of political experience and without any clear programme.

Moreover, as a teacher, he had betrayed "unprofessional" qualities: he enjoyed the *réclame* of his oratorical skill with his big classes, but disliked work with small groups. He was never at ease in personal contact, with academics or with business men. His view of politics was heavily pedagogic and declamatory, in an age when mass persuasion, without benefit of electronics, was one of the great tests. He had practised in his father's pulpit, haranguing the empty pews. Croly spoke of "his halo of shimmering rhetoric". His view of a political campaign was that of a series of speeches; and his success as a speaker hid from him that oratorical triumph is only a small part of the game. He was gifted with words and could project himself easily. But Lincoln Steffens made a shrewd distinction between his "wisdom" and that of House, and thought the latter's—essentially a form of political "know-how"—far more patient and productive in the end. Wilson came to lean on House, soft-spoken and endlessly obliging—"an intimate man", Jonathan Daniels put it, "even when cutting a throat". By the same token, he came to feel that it was this very skill of House's that had betrayed him at Paris.

Wilson saw himself less as a persuader than as a crusader, exhorter, and political evangelist. From this was derived, in part, his odd liking for Alexander Hamilton. The ideal was to be parliamentary: on the canal tolls question in 1913, he went so far as to threaten resignation unless Congress repealed the offending Act; in 1918, he sought a vote of confidence from the electorate. As

student, teacher, and politician, he preached the role of
the Presidency as a unifying force in government. He
appeared before Congress in person—reversing the
tradition that had held for over a century. By this
guidance of Congress and dramatisation of himself as
both legislator and executive, Wilson put through an
impressive amount of legislation in the halcyon days of
1912–14: the Clayton Anti-Trust Act, the Underwood
Tariff, the Federal Trade Commission, the Federal
Reserve Act. But these methods and achievements carried
their own penalty. Wilson was reluctant to share responsibility. He was irritated by opposition. He scorned the
advice of the military. By 1915 he had abandoned meetings with the Press. His advisers in foreign policy were
inexperienced; and all but Bryan were pro-British.

The appointment of Bryan to the Secretaryship of
State was in itself regarded as matter for alarm, a reward
for services rendered at the Baltimore Convention that
seemed to confirm the President's lack of interest in the
State Department. Bryan was discredited, both as man
and politician: a teetotaller, a fundamentalist, an agrarian
radical, and a party war-horse. His mind, said one cynic,
was like his native Platte River, "five inches deep and
five miles wide at the mouth". Assistant Secretary of
State Huntington Wilson reported that

> From the first moment his waiting room was over-
> flowing with political friends from all over the country
> seeking favour for themselves or their constituents. He
> was left hardly a moment for Department business and I
> even had to sign most of the mail for him. . . . He had
> never been interested in diplomacy; and this made it not

A.P.——G

only difficult but actually impossible quickly to impart to him a conception of foreign affairs.

If together Wilson and Bryan made a number of good appointments, twenty-nine of the forty-odd diplomatic chiefs of missions were changed within six months; and some distinguished career men—William Rockhill in Turkey, John B. Jackson in the Balkans, Arthur Beaupré in Cuba, William Russell in the Dominican Republic, and Percival Dodge in Panama—were removed. Wilson and Bryan got on happily together—more happily than might have been expected. The Canal Tolls exemption measure was repealed. Some twenty-two "cooling-off" treaties were signed. President and Secretary were in accord in their attitude to Dollar Imperialism—the proposed six-power consortium in China was repudiated. But the cooling-off treaties were of slight importance; before he left the White House, Wilson was to reverse himself on the role of the bankers in China; and in the Caribbean the United States Marines intervened in ways that suggested that Imperialism still flourished—the Roosevelt Corollary to the Monroe Doctrine was to be followed, it seemed, almost to the letter.

The two years from 1912 to 1914 brought one particularly revealing example of Wilson's strength and weakness. The Mexican affair and the frontier war it produced were a dramatic foretaste of things to come. Wilson began his Presidency with some impeccable liberal pronouncements. There was to be no emphasis on material or commercial motives, but on "the self-restraint of a really great nation which realises its own strength and scorns to misuse it". He declared at Mobile,

Alabama, in October 1913 that the United States would never acquire another square inch of territory at the expense of a neighbour. In keeping with this he refused to recognise the Huerta regime in Mexico. It was, he saw, "government by murder". The step seemed bold and liberal. In fact, it ran counter to the advice of the accredited American diplomats in Mexico City and the practice of all the other powers. It led him to send unofficial and less expert emissaries like John Lind. It encouraged rivals to Huerta like Carranza and Villa; it fostered civil confusion in Mexico and border war for years along the Mexican frontier; despite its intent, it led to the near-Imperialist actions at Tampico and Vera Cruz. War itself was only averted by the intervention of the ABC Powers[2] and the Niagara Falls Conference. And, by demanding the creation of "honest constitutional government" as a prerequisite to American recognition— teaching the world to elect good men, as he put it—a most dangerous precedent was set in the matter of recognition that has marked American policy ever since—towards Russia in 1917, towards the Kaiser in 1918, and towards China in 1949. Since 1913, American policy and world affairs have been bedevilled by Wilson's didacticism.

Whatever their value as the high point of Progressivism in domestic politics, the first two years were far from happy as auguries of "moral imperialism" abroad. The policy was negative; and all it had to its credit was the check to Dollar Diplomacy in China. This left the situation in China all but unchanged, as Madame Chiang Kai-Shek stressed in her own essay on Wilson

[2] Argentina, Brazil, Chile.

(*The Greatness of Woodrow Wilson*, ed. Alsop); Mexico was left in civil confusion; and the Marines were in Haiti and the Dominican Republic.

II

There is no evidence that Wilson judged the situation in Europe, on the outbreak of war in 1914, any more accurately than his countrymen. It was a war attributable to wicked men, to autocracy, and to the absence of genuinely democratic government, a war "whose causes cannot touch us". He shared the faith of the Progressives: man in America was a rational being, and war was barbarous; the American ethic was still a product of the farm, individualist, Utopian, and non-military; her only Imperialist philosopher thus far was a sailor, Mahan, not a soldier; separated from, and superior to, the feuds of the Old World, the United States could and should stay out. As late as February 1916, Wilson described American neutrality as "a matter of conviction and of the heart". This viewpoint was not far from that of the *Chicago Herald*, which offered a vote of thanks to Columbus for having discovered America.

Despite the testing issues of the first few months of the war—the bombing of Rheims and the German invasion of Belgium, with their sharp impact on American opinion ("Germany has almost made England popular in America", said Spring-Rice in October), the disputes with Britain over neutral shipping, over contraband and the seizure of mails and the black-listing of shipping firms— Wilson held to his faith in neutrality "in thought as well as in action". It came gradually to be reinforced by the hope that a free and neutral United States, growing in moral and material strength as the war dragged on, might in the end act, under his leadership, as an acceptable and impartial mediator.

It was to this end that House was sent on his three peace missions to Europe. When House, a far more realistic politician, returned in the spring of 1916 with the House–Grey memorandum, involving, if the proposed peace conference failed, a promise of American entry into war, Wilson retreated from such a step and added a cautionary "probably" to House's commitments. As late as September 1916, Wilson was so irritated by Britain that he got authority from Congress to prohibit loans and restrict exports to the allies if they did not change their policy. In January 1917, he still thought that the United States could and should remain aloof. Although it was hit upon by accident, Martin Glynn's slogan, "He kept us out of war", was a true statement. "Once lead the people into war and they'll forget there ever was such a thing as tolerance." If he lost this fight too, he fought hard and nobly for neutrality.

As always, the problem for the statesman was not the soundness of his aim but whether he could translate it into action: means, not ends, are the vital thing. If neutrality was the goal, how successful were the means? One difficulty here has often been cited—Wilson's Anglophilia. His ancestry and his Presbyterianism, his training as constitutional historian and political scientist—a training that had not included the customary spell in Germany—his love for the Lake poets, all ministered to a pro-British feeling. He certainly disliked the arbitrary character of the German Government and its militarism. Those who were close to him had no doubts about the depth of the private sympathy for Britain. " 'You and Grey are fed on the same food, and I think you understand.' There were tears in his eyes, and I am sure we can at the right moment depend upon an understanding heart here." So Spring-Rice wrote to Grey on 8 Sep. 1914. Of his advisers, only Bryan was strictly neutral, and he lacked the standing to make his neutrality impressive; anyway he resigned on the *Lusitania* question (May 1915). Walter Hines Page in London was more British than the British; Franklin Lane, his all-too-genial Secretary of the Interior, was a Canadian by birth; Lansing, who succeeded Bryan, became more and more critical of Germany—though more critical, perhaps, in his retrospective writings than in his actual administration; House by the spring of 1916, at least, if not much earlier, had come down on the British side.

But it is altogether too simple, and quite out of character, to see Wilson, the man of principle, finally falling victim to his own prejudices or those of his associates. He fought against these with Calvinist firmness. Alone they would never have determined his actions. Far more challenging than his pro-British sympathy was the dilemma presented by the situation in Europe, the succession of crises, the growing involvement. The theme of his career is this constant battle between ideal and reality, the all-too-wide gulf between his abstract principles and the difficulties and contradictions of the situation in which he found himself; and, on each occasion, it was his inflexible principles that were destroyed, and in the end the man with them. There was nothing wrong with the policy of neutrality, which clearly accorded with the wishes and economic interests of the majority of the American people. But, by restating in each crisis a position of principle, by giving no room to himself or to his emissaries to manœuvre, he inadvertently steered his country closer and closer to a point at which no alternative but war would remain open to it. As he put it to Senator Stone in 1916, "I cannot consent to any abridgement of the rights of American citizens in any respect . . . if in this instance we allowed expediency to take the place of principle, the door would inevitably be opened to still further concessions." This very firmness ministered to tension. The years from 1914 to April 1917 saw a succession of crises with common characteristics: they were invariably defined by him not as issues of peace *versus* war, but of morality *versus* expediency. Each time of course morality won; and each time war was remorselessly brought a step nearer.

The first step to perdition was the American note on "strict accountability" holding Germany responsible for any American vessels sunk or lives lost after she had proclaimed her submarine blockade of Britain in February 1915. The viewpoint was buttressed by the *Lusitania* notes in May, June, and July: submarine warfare violated the principles of international law, of humanity and justice; American citizens had a legal right to take passage on belligerent ships; international law provided for the safety of passengers and crew; any repetitions of the *Lusitania* sinking would be treated as an unfriendly act.

Bryan's refusal to sign the second of the *Lusitania* notes and his resignation dramatised Wilson's dilemma. He was seeking to argue not only that the sea-lanes should be peaceful avenues for Americans on their own ships, but that their presence on unarmed belligerent ships should make those ships sacrosanct. There can be no question that submarine warfare violated international law; there is some ground for wonder that the *Lusitania* should have been given no convoy or protection by Britain in the war zone; it is probable that, as he claimed, the commander of U-boat 20 did not know the name of his victim until he saw it on the ship's bows as she was sinking. Nevertheless, all this said, the decisions of February and May–July 1915 made the final steps inevitable, as Bryan—and the Germans—recognised.[3]

The decision to resume submarine warfare in January 1917 was taken by Germany in the full knowledge of the consequences: Wilson had made his position plain to Bernstorff and all concerned. But his stand had not averted war; and, had he been so minded, by accepting Bryan's position in 1915 or by accepting the Gore–McLemore Resolution in February 1916, he could at least have kept Americans from the high seas. In this sense, Wilson's rigidity on principle, the "fight" for justice in 1915 and 1916—like his "fight" at Princeton against living Deans and the dead hand of millionaires—was having inevitable consequences. He could have warned Americans against travel on the armed ships of

[3] Cf. T. A. Bailey, "The Sinking of the Lusitania", in *American Historical Review*, XLI (1935–6); "German Documents relating to the Lusitania", *Journal of Modern History*, VIII (1936).

belligerent powers; he could have ordered his own ships to avoid the war zones established by the belligerents; he could have swallowed whatever injuries or insults might have followed from such precautions. Such courses, however, were for him inconceivable: for American rights and honour were at issue; and on these there could be no compromise.

Not only American rights, but by 1916 the rights of all mankind were at issue. Had Wilson limited himself to defending Americans, and sought, ignobly perhaps, to keep them out of mischief, he might have averted war. But by 1916 he was taking a step beyond the question of submarine warfare and the role of neutrals, and he was presenting his arguments on it to the American people in new—and dangerously general—terms. The "preparedness" campaign of February 1916—in part wished upon him by his party with an eye on Republican charges in an election year, in part a necessary warning lest House's mission fail—was put to the American people by one who now saw himself as a crusader for world causes. "There is something that the American people love better than they love peace." "There is a price which is too great to pay for peace." The words are repeated in speech after speech: "moral obligation laid upon us"; "there are . . . rights higher and greater than the rights of trade and commerce. I mean the rights of mankind"; "we are in some sort and by the force of circumstances the responsible spokesmen of the rights of humanity." He put the case for "an universal association" of nations at a meeting of the League to Enforce Peace in 1916—sharing the platform, oddly enough, with Cabot Lodge. As late as

January 1917, the hope was still for neutrality. But another Wilson was appearing, now voicing principles not only of national honour but of international order.

If Wilson contributed by his inflexibility to the ultimate declaration of April 1917, the responsibility for American entry rests squarely on the German decision to resume submarine warfare, and on the singular folly of appealing to Mexico in the Zimmermann Note. If German calculations on U-boats were made coldly, they were not well served by their Intelligence in the United States; Admiral von Holtzendorf doubted if a single American soldier would set foot in Europe. By 1917 it was the German Government that was at once inflexible and rash.

Nor is there reason to assess the economic or propagandist pressures on Wilson. If the American economy was by 1917 in the broadest sense bound up with Allied victory, and if the pressures of Wall Street on public opinion and on Congress were considerable, there is little sign of financial pressures being brought to bear on Wilson. It was difficult enough for his closest Cabinet colleagues to influence him, much less Wall Street. "I rarely consult anybody", he told Ida Tarbell in 1916. And it is impossible to view the promoter of the Underwood Tariff, or of the Federal Reserve Act, as one ready to indulge in war to protect the investments of "privilege" and of "Other People's Money". Whatever the motives of Congress in 1917—at least as seen from the standpoint of Senator Nye in 1935—Wilson did not go to war to save the skins of bankers. Nor are the arguments of "Propaganda for War" any more convincing. It was the sound adage of the propagandists of World War II that no nation can be persuaded by propaganda to do something that it would not do anyway: all propaganda can do is to speed the process of conversion. The issues used by British propaganda between 1915 and 1917—used very skilfully, it is true—were provided by Germany; Bernstorff put the "blame" squarely on the German Foreign Office, not on Parker or Wiseman, on British Information Services or Admiral Hall and his cipher experts. There were forces at work here in economics and public opinion: but their importance has been exaggerated; and they certainly had little influence on Wilson himself.

What brought the United States into World War I was the German decision to resume U-boat warfare. That decision produced war, in part because of Wilson's stand on principle from February 1915. As late, however, as January 1917, he was hopeful of averting war. He might still have done so, had he been able to control one situation five thousand miles from American shores. The German decision of January 1917 might not have been made if the Russian Revolution had occurred two months earlier and had brought Germany victory on the eastern front. Coming when it did, however, with the United States indignant, and American lives being lost on the high seas, the Russian Revolution made it appear that the Allies—and their new Associate—were fighting the battle of democracy against autocracy. And here, after the failure to keep his country neutral, was a new battle to fight and a new crusade to lead—the greatest of them all.

III

The decision to go to Paris in person in 1918—about which there has been so much debate—was for Wilson itself a logical result of the decision to go to war in April 1917. If the world was to be re-made, it could only be done in Europe. And it was indeed only in the months in Paris, when he was almost at the end of his physical and nervous resources, that Wilson came to make any compromise with his principles. To Paris he went as a Messiah, cheered by returning troops as the *George Washington* sailed down the Hudson, fêted in London, Paris, and Rome, his image worshipped—for a time—in little shrines in Northern Italy. By the time of his return, though the crowds were out in Washington, so were his enemies in the Senate; the high idealism soon cooled in Europe and at home; and the Capitol was but dimly lit for his homecoming. The great test of Wilson, as negotiator, diplomat, and President, was his conduct abroad and at home from January to September 1919.

Hailed as saviour though he was on his arrival in Europe, Wilson was already a heavily committed politician. There was bitterness among Allied leaders that the German offer to negotiate had been made to Wilson; by his notes to the German Government, it was felt, he had allowed a peace mood to develop in Germany that threw awry the careful plans of the soldiery for a knock-out blow in the spring of 1919, and thus saved Germany from invasion and unconditional surrender. Germany itself was afterwards to make quite contradictory criticisms; that, far from being saved, she was offered conditions that were not in fact fulfilled, that she had been lured into a false confidence in Wilson's ability to carry out his undertakings. Out of this came the myth that she was not defeated in the field. Wilson had even sharper troubles with the Allies. The basis of negotiations with Germany was the Fourteen Points speech of January 1918. Yet, until November, the Allies had treated these with scant respect and had refused to approve them. Lloyd George never accepted the second clause committing the Allies to the freedom of the seas; and Clemenceau insisted on reparations from Germany for war damage to civilian populations. It is even doubtful if, before the armistice, Clemenceau had ever read the Fourteen Points speech. Only on House's insistence had the Fourteen Points been accepted by the Allies as a basis for the armistice; and this approval had led to the so-called "Pre-Armistice Agreement".

Moreover, the awe in which Wilson was held by the European crowds was not shared by their more cynical leaders. Clemenceau's savage references to Wilson's piety and moralism are well known—"he speaks like Jesus Christ but he acts like Lloyd George" was only one of his pleasantries; Wilson's confrères in Paris were shrewd judges of a politician's strength and weaknesses; newspapers as sympathetic to Wilson as the London *Times* had already been speaking of "the reign of righteousness". And, by January 1919, there were many gaps in Wilson's political and personal armour. His ill-judged appeal for the return of Democrats in the Congressional elections of November 1918 had failed; the Republicans had a majority of two in the Senate; and the control of the Senate Foreign Relations Committee had passed into the hands of his bitter critic, Henry Cabot Lodge; it was possible for European politicians to see Wilson as one already repudiated at home.

His peace commission—General Tasker Bliss, Lansing, House, Henry White, and Wilson himself— was thoroughly unrepresentative; it included neither a Senator nor a major Republican—White, the sole Republican, was an ex-Ambassador of small influence in Republican circles. Wilson brought with him to Europe a cohort of advisers, many of them selected from the group known as the Inquiry; and he needed a liner to carry them. There were distinguished figures in this intelligence service, from its head, Sidney Mezes of the College of the City of New York, House's brother-in-law, to its youthful secretary, Walter Lippmann; and they included some academic figures who then and later were to be among the outstanding men of their day— James Shotwell, Isaiah Bowman, Charles Seymour, and C. H. Haskins, to name only a few. It was Lippmann and the journalist Frank Cobb who drafted that "interpretation" of the Fourteen Points that became Wilson's working guide at Paris. Yet this assistance, expert though it might be, was not weighty in influencing the Senate or the House back home; and it was not particularly effective in quickly pre-digesting material for Wilson's use in Paris. Harold Nicolson has left a scathing indictment of Wilson and the American delegation at work in his *Peacemaking 1919*.

With some of his advisers Wilson was to have sharp differences of opinion—as over Italy; and they did not save him from revelations of profound ignorance of history and geography. Somewhat casually, he had already "created" certain "new" countries,—like Czecho-slovakia; he only afterwards learnt of the size of the German population in northern Bohemia. His faith in national self-determination was hard to translate into reasonable terms for the populations of Eastern Europe. He was never very certain about his Near Eastern geography; and he had a perennial difficulty over the location of Baghdad. If his confusion over the status of the Tigris–Euphrates valley was in 1919 all too under-standable—and reflected, be it said, the contemporary confusion in Baghdad itself—his frequent inaccuracies and vagueness augured ill for the bigger inquest ahead of him at home.

Knowledge of the idealism but vagueness of Wilson's approach, and of his somewhat amateur intelligence service, was perhaps among the reasons why Colonel House, who had spent a few months in Europe as his emissary, had urged him not to come to Paris in person. In House's view—and Seymour's—this was his supreme mistake. "He was the *God on the Mountain*," wrote House, "and his decisions regarding international matters were practically final. When he came to Europe and sat in conference with the Prime Ministers and representatives of other states, he gradually lost his place as first citizen of the world." House and Lansing both urged him not to attend—and House reported that his view was supported by Reading, Wiseman, and Clemenceau. This may well have begun the process of Wilson's own disenchantment with House himself; by March 1919 he came to discern

and dislike House's own easy acceptance by the French
and the British, to be sensitive about House's conferences
with them, to feel that House was "giving away" all he
had stood for.

Wilson's difficulties at Paris, however, were, in the
last analysis, a matter of personality. He distrusted even
his closest advisers; and, after his quick visit to the
United States in February–March 1919, the distrust
deepened. It brought a break with House; and in the end
the break was complete. He refused to see House again
after he left Paris and House never could discover why.
As the conference progressed, he relied more and more
on the rightness of his own judgment, and more and more
drew on his own reserves for assurance. White, once
Ambassador in Paris, was never used as an intermediary
with Clemenceau. Wilson took the decision to send
troops to Siberia without discussion with his Secretary
of War, Newton D. Baker—though Baker was his
favourite Cabinet officer. The view that he had expressed
on the *George Washington en route* to Europe, that he
would be the only disinterested member of the Conference because he had no territorial demands to make or
reparations to ask, grew in certainty as the months
passed. None of his advisers could obtain specific or
concrete statements from him. His frankness in stating
his views, at the outset of an argument, made retreat
difficult; for the retreat was always so much an abandon-
ment of a very general principle. Anything other than
firmness, however, became, in his eyes, a form of
surrender. To bargain was to play a European—and an
immoral—game. Lloyd George described him as "a

missionary whose function it was to rescue the poor
European heathen from their age-long worship of false
and fiery gods". This remained the fundamental tragedy
in Wilson—a tragedy bound up with his own fineness of
character and transparent honesty of intention—the
belief, so close to naïveté, that there was a right in
politics of which he alone was the champion. "Tell me
what is right and I'll fight for it" was a dangerously
simple view to bring to a war-torn world in 1919. Parliamentary politicians had long lost such illusions.

Moreover, Wilson was at a tactical disadvantage
vis-à-vis Lloyd George, Clemenceau, and Orlando. They
were wilier men than he; and they were certainly more
adept in the ways of the *coulisses*. Wilson had the dis-
advantages of one over-dependent on the document and
the printed word. He stayed up night after night wrestling
with written material, in a constantly losing effort to keep
pace with the problems that awaited him next day; his
associates—whom he was prompt to see as enemies quite
as tangible as the Germans—were far better trained in
learning from conversation and from quick summaries,
and were better acquainted with the nature of the
problems themselves. He had only two stenographers
at the Conference, had made no plans for adequate
secretarial staff, and made far from efficient use of the
service House provided for him. Once again, Wilson had
to draw on his reserves of nervous and mental energy.
"The rest of us", said Lloyd George years later, "found
time for golf and we took Sundays off, but Wilson,
in his zeal, worked incessantly." Soon there came testi-
ness and ill-concealed anger; in April came influenza

A.P.—H

and conversations through bedroom-doors; occasionally there were evidences of utter tactlessness—in the failure to voice appreciation of the sufferings of Britain or France, the brusque refusal to visit the battlefields or devastated areas of Northern France, or the folly of the Fiume appeal to the Italian people over the heads of their chosen leaders. The errors have their own nobility—the high temper and will-power of an over-worked and over-dedicated man, fighting against error and wickedness that he was prompt to see personified in those about him. The admirer of Bagehot refused to accept, as binding on himself, the master's respect for a liberal society as "a polity of discussion". For him, politics was an affair of *pronunciamentos*.

This, however, is not to say that Wilson failed at Paris. A critic might even argue that it was only his brusqueness and inflexibility that won any concessions from the selfish European politicians. He had not achieved all his Fourteen Points: but without them the Treaty would have been a great deal worse than it was. He had wanted a fixed amount of reparations to be agreed on, and a definite type of payment specified. There were to be no "punitive damages". He had been compelled to accept the inclusion of the cost of pensions in addition to direct damages: but he had at least succeeded in keeping the demands made on Germany short of the total costs of the war. By promising an aid to France that the Senate later was to ban, he prevented the complete separation of the Rhineland from Germany, and the annexation of the Saar by France. He had the ex-German colonies "mandated" to the League, and thus probably speeded the process whereby they are reaching their ultimate independence. If he lost to the Japanese on Shantung, at least he extracted a promise of the eventual return of sovereignty over Shantung to China. If it was far from the idyllic hopes of December, the Treaty agreed on in May 1919 was, as Wilson put it to Ray Stannard Baker, "the best that could be had out of a dirty past". This is what Charles Seymour has in mind when he refers to "the Paris education" of Wilson.

And, for Wilson, the gloom was offset by the creation of the League of Nations. It had been set up with astonishing ease by a Commission over which he had himself presided; the Covenant was drafted, and approved by a plenary Conference, before his visit to Washington was made in February; and to all the mounting problems of the period after March—consequent on what R. S. Baker described over-dramatically as the February "plot"—it was in the League that Wilson put his faith. The more difficult the issues to be resolved, the more there would be for the League to do. His very success here contrasting with the battle of words with Lodge and the Round Robin of the dissenting Senators before he sailed back to Paris, brought both exaltation and exasperation. The Covenant became bound up with the Treaty and with the man—a symbol of his European achievement.

IV

Despite Lodge and the die-hards, the attitude in Washington towards the League and the Treaty in July

1919 was not hostile. Most Democrats and most Republicans supported it; so did Taft and Root. There is no
reason to doubt Seymour's view that "a few conciliatory
gestures by the President would have sufficed to win the
two-thirds vote necessary to ratification". They were
not forthcoming. He acted gracelessly and, in its eyes,
unconstitutionally towards the Senate, and peremptorily
towards its Foreign Relations Committee. On Colonel
House's pressing, he gave a dinner to the Senate and
House Committees; he thought it unsuccessful. Senator
Brandegee said it was like wandering with Alice in
Wonderland and having tea with the Mad Hatter. For
Wilson there would be no changes in Covenant or
Treaty—even though Grey brought evidence later that
Europe would have been ready to accept any changes the
Senate thought necessary. By September, Wilson saw the
issue as sharp and personal, a battle between himself and
Lodge. Once again, the people should be the judge.
Once more, the liberal optimism held, and for the last
time. "Whoever knew truth put to the worse in free and
open encounter?"

On 3 Sep. 1919 Wilson set out, against his doctor's
orders, on his famous crusade in the West; thirty-seven
speeches in twenty-three days, and the last the greatest of
all. "My clients are the children", he said. "My clients are
the next generation." But, on 25 September, at Pueblo,
Colorado, when he thought the tide was turning towards
him in the country, he reached the limit of his nervous
and physical strength. Brought back to Washington, he
suffered a stroke on 2 October, and for seven and a half
months conducted no official business. He was guarded

with possessive, even perhaps over-zealous, devotion by his wife—the second wife, Edith Bolling Galt, whom he had married in December 1915. Only four or five people were allowed to visit him. So complete was the isolation, that a Senate and House Committee had to insist on seeing him—"the smelling Committee", as Wilson called it, led by one of his critics, the opprobrious Senator Fall. Whatever the cause, however vigilant Mrs Wilson might be, there was no leadership from the White House; and there could be no compromise. He had been forced into compromises at Paris, and had emerged with some results to show. He might have done so once more in Washington, had he been fit. But, leaderless, his Democratic Senators held to an all-or-nothing attitude, enough, in alliance with the dozen irreconcilables in the Senate, to prevent the necessary two-thirds majority. This was not Lodge's fault, in November at least; he was for the Treaty, heavily amended. The Democrats, uncritically loyal to their stricken master, would not budge. In November the Treaty, with the Lodge reservations attached, was defeated (55:39). In March 1920 it had a majority, but this was seven short of the necessary two-thirds. Irony was added to tragedy by the fact that, in the end, the Treaty was defeated not by its enemies but by its friends.

The fault was hardly Wilson's, since he was *incommunicado*; he had made his contribution to the result, however, by his earlier intransigence. Lodge had contributed, by a political tactic that was quite remarkable; for it had succeeded by March 1920 in undoing what in November some eighty per cent of Americans had wanted. And Lodge had done this by an uncanny skill in reading Wilson's mind, and assuming its inflexibility. Only an emissary close to Wilson's heart could now have acted as an interpreter of his obstinacy, his dedication, and his faith. But House was not permitted an entrance. The circle of friends was now very small. And the democracy that depended so heavily on the leader drifted under Harding towards isolation and Normalcy. For the next three years Wilson led a retired life, a crippled figure in a bath-chair. He died on 3 Feb. 1924.

The defeat was that of Wilson and the League, far more than that of the Treaty of Versailles. Indeed, when in the end the United States made its peace with Germany by the Treaty of Berlin (August 1921), it did so by incorporating into that Treaty many of the less happy terms of the Treaty of Versailles. The United States accepted the decisions on colonies and reparations, on war-guilt and on the military occupation of Germany. What it rejected were, in fact, the more constructive aspects—the League and the International Labour Organisation—although, here again, the reality was less disturbing than the myth, and to many League conferences it sent observers, and joined the I.L.O. in 1934. What was rejected in 1919 and 1920 was Wilsonian idealism and Wilson's effort at justice, and the risky ventures of Article X.[4] The United States was not acting from motives of a superior morality; it was being neither noble nor isolationist, but at best cautious, and at worst

[4] Article X of the League of Nations Charter was an attempt to guarantee the territorial status quo against aggression.

blindly vindictive. It, too, had cried for revenge against Germany; and by the terms of the 1921 Treaty it was quite as responsible as any other Power, in law and morality, for the events that unfolded in Europe. All it had done was to weaken the one institution, which its own President had laboured to build, that might have been able to control them.

One has then not to look far to understand the reasons for the lack of a Wilson legend. Failure alone would not prevent its growth—though, as with everything in politics, it is success that breeds admiration and anecdote. But legends are part of folklore; and Wilson remains not only an idealist who failed but a forbidding figure. His ways now seem cold, and his language stilted and pious. Even the efforts to present him as warm and human, dancing a jig on station platforms in the 1912 campaigns, coaching the football squad, composing limericks and telling dialect stories, read oddly in our own world, at once more folksy and more sophisticated. What fun there may have been was less in evidence after 1912, and especially after his wife's death in 1914. The academic turned politician is seen to have been from the first more politician than academic; despite the record as student and as teacher, his range of learning was narrow, his tastes administrative rather than original. He made few contributions to his chosen field, domestic reform; what he voiced was familiar. He made no attempt to solve the racial question, or to check the Red Scare, caused largely by his own Attorney-General, Mitchell Palmer. The crusade against the special interests and against "privilege" was rooted in a faith in the judgment of the people that it is now harder to accept than it was then. He applied it lavishly, and sometimes disastrously, at the expense of other people's leaders in Mexico and Italy, in ways that showed a grave lack of patience and an incapacity to appraise political realities. There was an undercurrent of national pride in Wilson that marks him of the age of Burgess, Mahan, and T.R.: there was not so much to choose between the *New Nationalism* and the *New Freedom*—and neither of them was very new. After each initial success in his career—as professor, as Governor, as President—came a reaction and some degree of failure. On each occasion he escaped and started afresh elsewhere. The ideals were of the highest: but each time the edifice crumbled in his hands.

The greatest defeat of all—over American entry into the League—is now seen in the light of our own experience since 1946 not to have mattered so much anyway; international organisation is no longer seen as the great panacea for the world's ills. It is now generally agreed that, if Wilson was not the most culpable figure in the great debate in 1919, by his intransigence he made compromise impossible. And psychologists, as well as historians, have seen deep personal malaise in the man's loneliness, his frequent headaches, his need for women friends, the speed of his second marriage, the final break with House and Tumulty. He never lived at peace with himself, says Garraty. Some psychologists have argued that it was his personal maladjustment that bred the driving energy and ambition. "I want people to love me," Wilson said, "but I suppose they never will." The incapacity to elicit affection, for which he strove harder

History Today

Woodrow Wilson at Columbus, Ohio, 4 Sep. 1919.

Woodrow Wilson and

Keystone Press Agency

King Albert of the Belgians.

Navy Secretary, Joseph Daniels, presenting F. D. Roosevelt with a loving cup, when the latter left his post as Assistant Secretary to begin his campaign for the Vice-Presidency.

than most, is in the end the reason why there is here little material for legend.

This is, however, not the final verdict; for verdicts reflect our own age and our own needs. In 1940 and 1941 Wilson was seen by Paul Birdsall as one who "With all his mistakes, . . . emerges as the only man of real stature at Paris." The case for intervention in 1917 is now made less in terms of Wilsonian idealism, British propaganda, or American bankers, than as a matter of sober self-interest, as by Lippmann and Buehrig. It is no longer seen as a matter for controversy; and Wilson's own anxious heart-searching is minimised—as is his long fight to keep the United States out of war. Wilson at Paris is judged by the now professional standards of cold-war diplomacy, and in the light of the disillusion that attaches to much international action. He thought that he had but to declare his truths for the people—in the United States in 1912 or 1916, in Germany in 1917, and in Italy in 1919— to heed his call. Even for Clemenceau this was *noble candeur*. Today his idealism is even more clearly out of fashion. Yet few would challenge the man's integrity, his honesty, or his battle for what he thought was right. The criticisms made of him are primarily criticisms of method. Even his failure to realise what Salvador de Madariaga called "the dream of reason"—as, in the short view, a failure it must be described—has the elements of Greek or Roman tragedy about it. His career, like that of Coriolanus, is far nobler in its defeat than the success stories of many lesser men.

THE ROOSEVELT REVOLUTION
OF 1933–38[1]

There was a youngster once who told his father that the teacher wanted him to bring to school simple statements of the Einstein theory and of the New Deal. "We will begin with the Einstein theory," said his father, "it is easier."

That this is a story Herbert Hoover liked to tell does not invalidate it as a commentary on the present state of the historical assessment of the New Deal years. Despite the vantage point of thirty years, and all that has passed since, the more that is written on the New Deal, the more blurred becomes the picture. Thirty years ago one of the first studies appeared—Ernest Lindley's *The Roosevelt Revolution*. Since then journalists and reporters, associates and bitter enemies have poured out volumes. There are some two hundred and eighty of them. Now that the vast collection of papers at Hyde Park, weighing at least forty tons, is open to historians, the large-scale "life and times" are appearing. Alongside them are the Public Papers. The process of clarification, burdened by the size of the archive, is not being greatly helped by the addiction of contemporary writers to hero-worship and to the quest for historical parallels. Mr Arthur Schlesinger, Junior, whose earlier study of the Jackson of the 1830s was itself largely conditioned by a particular view of the

[1] [Originally published in *History Today*, XII (1962), pp. 821-32.]

labour movement of the 1930s, does not hide his admiration for Franklin Delano Roosevelt in the three volumes of political and intellectual history that he has thus far written under the title *The Age of Roosevelt*. With more restraint, Professor Freidel of Harvard is similarly moved in his more conventionally-shaped biography. And the trend does not stop with the New Deal or with 1945. Many of President Kennedy's lieutenants, chosen like Franklin D. Roosevelt's Brain Trust from the faculties of New England Universities (F.D.R. at least chose them from more than one institution), judged the circumstances of 1961 by the stereotype of 1933. "The task of 1961", said Schlesinger, then historian-in-residence to President Kennedy, "was to complete F.D.R.'s 'unfinished business.' But the New Deal was a response to economic collapse, mass unemployment, stark hunger. What Kennedy faces is an invisible crisis. Troubles are here but they're not felt in the lives of many ordinary Americans." Historical parallelism of this sort, except as an academic exercise, is a dangerous ploy, for there are few true analogies in history. No one President—or King or Prime Minister— can be compared or contrasted with another without a vast degree of blindness to all the factors, great and small, that have changed in the interim. All that we know about the future, to coin a phrase, is that it will be different from the past. Despite this truism, the Roosevelt legend has for Democrats become so compelling that many of them now see the events of the present in the dazzling light of the Roosevelt years.

Two aspects of Roosevelt's career are of small

relevance to any attempt to assess the early New Deal in the light of what historians are making of it: his life up to 1920, and his foreign policy in and after 1940. To the British observer these two issues bulk, of course, very prominently. By 1940 and certainly by 1941, Roosevelt had become a magical name in Britain, and it has been impossible ever since to minimise Britain's indebtedness to him. It is hardly too much to say that Britain survived the grim years from Dunkirk to Alamein on a diet of Churchill's magnificent oratory—a war weapon beyond price or assessment—and on a prescription by Churchill of Roosevelt's sympathy and ultimate help, a prescription, be it said, that was itself grounded on a guess about the future and not on a study of Roosevelt's policy in the past. As a result of this, and of his and his country's contribution after 1941, F.D.R. enjoys a place in Britain's affections that cannot be questioned. Not all Americans endorse the British esteem for his foreign policy. But this factor is not relevant to the New Deal years since, until 1937, Roosevelt had no distinct foreign policy at all. Not until 1937 did he suggest that hostility to the dictators was a permissible policy for his country. He allowed himself to act as late as 1940 within the confines of the Neutrality Acts. Equally, the story of the poor little rich boy cushioned by affluence, by the best education the United States could give, at Groton and Harvard, and by the chaperonage, even at Harvard, of a doting mother, is familiar, non-controversial and of small significance.

What, however, is relevant is his political apprenticeship. It is now clear that the polio from which he made so spirited a come-back in 1921 and afterwards was not a great water-shed in his political—although a tremendous and dreadful water-shed in his personal—life. There is no evidence for the view that polio purified his spirit and dedicated him as the prophet of the New Deal. His ambition was certainly steeled by the triumph of will-power over physical suffering. After his illness, says Rex Tugwell, he was a man of "unassailable confidence"; his jaw, it is said, took on a grimmer line and the boyish grin came less easily. But the ambition long preceded 1921. Born with every advantage, he had early decided on poli-tics, largely because of the glamour of the career of his fifth cousin, Theodore Roosevelt (Uncle Teddy). Being without a political philosophy, his choice of a party was it-self determined as much from calculation as from convic-tion: if Democratic Roosevelts were oddities, oddities in politics were themselves worth cultivating. If he got his foot on the first rung of the ladder by challenging Tammany—a Roosevelt perhaps could afford to do this? —he moved up to the second by coming to terms with it —an indulgence that a Roosevelt again could afford. Devoid of ideals, he could be devoid of illusions; the great game could be played for the fun and skill of it, for it was essentially a matter of who gets what, when, and how. As Professor Burns in his study of him, *The Lion and the Fox*, reveals, he was prompt to use every incident to build up a favourable image. Although as Assistant Secretary of the Navy in World War I he never got nearer to the front than an official tour of the battle area, he wrote to Groton when he heard that a World War tablet was being put up in the school chapel—"I believe that my name should go in the first division of those who were 'in the service', especially as I saw service on the other side, was missed by torpedoes and shells . . ." Even the shattering impact of polio at the age of thirty-nine was used to fit into the existing political stereotype: the flag-carrier, as Vice-Presidential candidate in 1920, was likely to be a candidate again; the picture of the fight back from crippling illness was itself of vote-gathering importance. During his illness he sent three thousand letters annually to politicians to keep his contacts alive; his wife became reporter and runner, eyes and ears. The pursuit of power was calculated and self-conscious. The readiness to be the nominator of Al Smith for the Presidency—and the grim physical struggle to be able to walk far enough unaided in order to do it—was part of it. The Governorship of New York State in 1928 was, beyond all else, a step towards the Presidency. And when in 1930 he was re-elected, Will Rogers (who himself got twenty-two wild votes at the Democratic Convention in 1932) prophesied it: "The Democrats nominated their President yesterday, Franklin D. Roosevelt."

Will Rogers was far more prescient than the professionals or the pundits. Walter Lippmann in January 1932 saw Roosevelt merely as "an amiable man with many philanthropic impulses . . . who without any important qualification for the office would very much like to be President". Edmund Wilson saw him as a politically immature Boy Scout. In 1928 when Al Smith heard that there was talk at party headquarters in New York of F.D.R. for Governor of the State, his comment was:

"Out of the question! You know as well as I do that
Frank hasn't any brains." Four years later, Smith was to
have even stronger reasons for displeasure. "He has
always been kind to me and my family", he told Clark
Howell of the Atlanta Constitution, "but"—Smith rose,
stamped and went on, "do you know, by God, that he has
never consulted me about a damn thing since he has been
Governor? He has taken bad advice from sources not
friendly to me. He has ignored me!"

The significance of the New Deal turns on three
phenomena: on Hoover and his measures; on F.D.R. and
his policy; and on the success of the latter. Recent writing
suggests that the old verdict, of a saviour appearing in
1933, will no longer serve.

First, Hoover. The Engineer of Prosperity has become
so identified with the failure of the mechanism in 1929
that any objective judgment is now very difficult to make.
The collapse of the lush and fantastic world of the
Twenties was so beyond all expectation and analysis that
it was inevitable to blame it on Hoover. Hoover himself
blamed it first on American overspeculation, but
eventually he put most of the responsibility on worsening
conditions in Europe and on the easy money policy that
European statesmen persuaded the American Government to adopt. John K. Galbraith, the Harvard economist,
who was President Kennedy's Ambassador in India,
saw the trouble as American rather than European,
rooted in an economy with too wide a gap between rich
and poor, with a banking system in which the weak units
could bring down the strong, and in which too few of

the experts were fully aware of what was happening. There were in fact a host of causes, domestic as well as foreign: war debts, reparations, currency manipulations, tariff barriers abroad, but also sick industries at home, such as coal and railways, under-consumption by urban workers and by farmers, technological unemployment caused by industrial advance itself, too much speculation in many industries, too little buying power among the public as a whole. What is certainly clear is that Hoover was not to blame, and if disaster had human agents, his predecessors in office were far more responsible than he was himself.

Hoover, however, had serious limitations in coping with a crisis that was, at least in part, a crisis of confidence as well as of the economic system. Of high ideals and considerable administrative capacity, his approach was that of the business man: like many a Republican standard-bearer before and since, he had never been a politician in the conventional or partisan sense. Like Willkie in 1940 or Eisenhower in 1952, he had never run for political office before he ran for the Presidency. At bottom he was a *laissez-faire* liberal, whose reputation rested, for Republicans, on his engineering skills; for others, on his reputation as a Wilsonian relief administrator in Europe. He had lived most of his life outside the United States—he thought pre-1914 England "the most comfortable place to live in the whole world". Mr Schlesinger speaks of his qualities as those of a doctrinaire—"Doctrinaire by temperament, he tended to make every difference in degree a difference in kind and to transform questions of tactics into questions of principles.

... His was the tragedy of a man of high ideals whose intelligence froze into inflexibility and whose dedication was smitten by self-righteousness."

There was a failure of imagination, best indicated in his expulsion of the Bonus Army from Anacostia Flats in Washington in 1932 and his refusal to see their leaders— an expulsion carried out by four troops of cavalry and infantry with bayonets and tear gas, forces commanded by General Douglas MacArthur and his aide, Major Dwight D. Eisenhower. This was a profound psychological, not to mention a human, failure. "Thank God", he rashly exclaimed during the 1932 campaign, "we still have a Government in Washington that knows how to deal with the mob." He defended the protective tariff and the gold standard as arks of the covenant. Yet, all this said, it is striking how far—if often with great reluctance—Hoover was prepared to go in meeting a situation so much beyond his imagining—or perhaps his control. It was Hoover who committed the White House to the first serious efforts to halt the depression. His Federal Farm Board attempted to support agricultural prices—but its resources proved quite inadequate. The Reconstruction Finance Corporation was set up to give Government assistance to business; and in the end he approved of federal loans from the Reconstruction Finance Corporation to the States. A Federal Home Loan Bank Act was passed on Hoover's urging to ease the mortgage-pressure on home-owners. He advocated the establishment of a Public Works Administration—but Congress refused to support him. Not merely did these measures presage the outline of the New Deal, there was

A.P.—I

during 1932 a clearer policy for coping with the crisis coming from Hoover than from Roosevelt. Compare the resounding generalities of Roosevelt—"The country needs, and, unless I mistake its temper, the country demands bold persistent experimentation"—and the specific recommendations to Congress, eighteen of them, that Hoover was able to point to in a campaign speech at Detroit in October 1932.

> Practically the only evidence of the Democratic candidate upon this programme is the sneer that it has been designed to help banks and corporations, that it has not helped the common man. He knows full well that the only purpose of helping an insurance company is to protect the policy-holder.

Indeed, in the nine months that then stretched between nomination in June and election in the following March, it was far from clear what Roosevelt intended. He had got the nomination only on the fourth ballot—and the Smith forces never made it unanimous. Having secured it, he was fully aware that the mood of 1932, with some fourteen million unemployed, made the defeat of Hoover all but certain: like Lincoln in 1860, having been nominated he could now hardly lose. And so while the talk was robust, its content was nebulous, even reactionary. He outdid Hoover in demands for economy cuts. He wanted a twenty-five per cent cut in the budget. To win the support of the isolationists he disowned one of the few altruistic decisions of his career—his support in 1920 for Wilson and the League. In his speeches there is hardly any reference to inflation, hardly any suggestion of pump priming. He held firm to the politician's golden rule, which he later expressed himself: "You know the first thing a President has to do in order to put through good legislation? He has to get elected." Yet once elected, in the four-month interregnum between November 1932 and March 1933, he refused all Hoover's requests for collaboration in dealing with the crisis. He went far to wreck the London Economic Conference. His target remained purely political; to square his critics and to settle accounts with his backers, he picked a Cabinet dominated by Conservatives and Southern reactionaries. Hoover did not and perhaps could not avert a catastrophe that he did not create. Nevertheless, he had already undermined Coolidge's faith that the business of America was business. The Government had, however reluctantly, intervened. *Laissez-faire* had been sabotaged by its own engineer. But the changes were niggling and unconvincing, the engineer ashamed and without hope. He was, he said, at the end of his tether. He lacked, and Roosevelt had in abundance, political flair and political confidence. Roosevelt certainly stood for a more positive government than Hoover's, but he did not reveal how he would use his positive powers. Hoover's distaste for his successor can be amply understood.

Second, Roosevelt and his policy. Until March 1933, he did not know what it was himself. Even the phrase "The New Deal" was derivative and, significantly, a merger of Theodore Roosevelt's Square Deal and Wilson's New Freedom. The phrase itself was coined just before the acceptance speech at Chicago. It was set

A.P.—I*

down by Rosenman without a full understanding of how
it would stick, like Eisenhower's pledge that he would, if
elected, go to Korea and end the war. "If you were to be
nominated tomorrow and had to start a campaign trip
within ten days," Rosenman had told Roosevelt in
March 1932, "we'd be in an awful fix." To provide a
policy for the campaign, Rosenman had persuaded him
to call in professors. If business men were failing, could
dons and intellectual brokers be any worse? And so they
came: Raymond Moley, Rex Tugwell, Adolf Berle the
first of them, with Sammy "the Rose" and Henry "the
Morgue" (Henry Morgenthau) and with Ernest Lindley,
of the *New York Herald Tribune*, helping as speech
writer. Sherwood and McLeitch, Corcoran and Frankfurter, and social workers such as Frances Perkins and
Harry Hopkins, were to follow. Yet the gathering and
shaping of ideas were frighteningly casual. "We could
throw out pieces of theory", Tugwell wrote later. "We
could suggest relations; and perhaps the inventiveness of
the suggestion would attract his notice. But the tapestry
of the policy he was weaving was guided by an artist's
conception which was not made known to us." When
Tugwell devised his programme for agriculture—
essentially that of restricting production to send up
prices, a device of enforced restrictionism—he had
difficulty in explaining it on the telephone to F.D.R.
F.D.R. brought in Rosenman who could not understand
it either. "Well, Professor," said Roosevelt finally, "put
it in a telegram—two or three hundred words—and
we'll work it into the speech. I'll take your word for it
that it's the latest and most efficient model."

By March 1933, with the doors of every bank in the country closed, the President was committed to every policy under the sun. Even his final election speech in reply to Hoover's in November had been a merger of three men's drafts, with an introduction of his own. When asked to choose between ideas propounded from opposed camps like free trade and protection, his solution, offered with gusto and his own inimitable charm, was: "Fine! Fine! Weave the two together."

For the essence of Roosevelt's political flair lay in his ability as a fixer—of ideas as of men. He was not an original thinker. When he met Keynes, in so many ways the *fons et origo* of the ideas he was applying, he did not take to him and was out of his depth. Intellectually, he was far less prepared for his job than either Theodore Roosevelt or Wilson. And consistency for him was unimportant. He was fully aware where his skill—and his strength—lay. For in surrounding himself with men of strong personality who were endlessly clashing with each other, F.D.R. could himself reign as king, his *bonhomie* the balance-wheel of the Administration, his humour itself a weapon. He sought deliberately, it seems, to create areas of conflict in order to act as prince rather than prophet—arbiter between Hopkins and Ickes, Donald Nelson and Averell Harriman, Hull and Welles. Justice Holmes recognised the situation a few months after Roosevelt entered the White House: "a second-rate intellect but a first-rate temperament". It was temperament and faith in action—almost any action—by the Government that was the essence of the first New Deal.

Of action there was plenty in the first Hundred Days,

although the pattern set was highly inconsistent. A bank holiday was proclaimed, and the banks were put under licence: in the end, two thousand were compelled to close for ever; those that survived had the nation's confidence. The Glass–Steagall Act gave a federal guarantee to all bank deposits in the Federal Reserve System, and the governors of the Federal Reserve Board were given stronger powers of control of the nation's credit; commercial and investment banking were separated. Confidence in the national credit system was restored. The Home Owners' Loan Corporation went further than Hoover's measure in helping mortgagors; the Farm Credit Administration did the same for farmers. And the emphasis on economy was maintained: government expenditure was cut; even the Veterans Bureau was docked of some $300 million. These measures, like the abandonment of Prohibition, were in substance conservative.

The National Industry Recovery Act was perhaps the outstanding example of Roosevelt as an ideological fixer. It took over and made binding the business methods suggested by the United States Chamber of Commerce and already applied in the Twenties: the establishment of standards, the fixing of fair trade practices, and in some cases the actual fixing of prices. It satisfied, in other words, a business demand for Government approval of fair competition. But it tied this up with a similar demand on the part of the American Federation of Labour and the American labour movement for protection for the worker in the form of minimum wages and restrictions on hours of work. If, on the one hand, industry was to be

stimulated, labour was, on the other, to be protected—
and to be sure of its power to purchase the products of
industry. Codes of fair practices were to be drawn up
for each industry. And the right of collective bargaining
was guaranteed—bargaining to be done by representatives freely chosen by the employees. And even this was
a skilful piece of evasion, for it left the way open as much
to the company union as the trade union. The National
Recovery Administration, with the Blue Eagle as its
symbol and General Hugh Johnson as its vigorous and
often profane administrator, seemed a politician's master-
piece.

Nor can the Agricultural Adjustment Act be seen as
anything but an artificial device to maintain prices by
scarcity. In return for a restriction of output, farmers were
offered benefit payments on cotton, wheat, corn, pigs,
tobacco, and rice. To meet the cost of this, a processing
tax was levied on these staples. Since crops were already
in the ground, the Government went further and
ordered the deliberate ploughing under of a portion of the
cotton crop and the slaughter of more than six million
pigs. And a curious new concept was introduced, the
idea of parity: the price received by the farmer was to be
equal to the purchasing power of agricultural com-
modities in the years 1909–14. The Government now,
in fact, supported a planned agriculture and in sub-
sidising non-production seemed to support a planned
capitalism in reverse. "Hoover proposed to plough up
every fourth row of cotton", orated the Kingfish in
Louisiana. "Roosevelt went him one better and ploughed
up every third row."

If much in this programme can be seen as a series of devices for maintaining the capitalist system, if system it was, there were many features of the first New Deal that brought alarm, even panic, to capitalists. The Government went off the gold standard. It introduced the Securities Exchange Commission to supervise the financial market. The Tennessee Valley Authority was set up—the most controversial of all Roosevelt's early measures, although now seen in retrospect as one of the most valuable. And there was a vast relief programme— in the Public Works Administration run by atrabilious and testy Harold Ickes, the Civil Works Administration of Harry Hopkins and the Civilian Conservation Corps. These won support from labour and the unemployed: but they were anathema to business.

And how successful was this "first" New Deal? In law, most unsuccessful. Both N.I.R.A. and A.A.A. were declared invalid by the Supreme Court. Nor, as a principle of Government policy, was planning successful. Raymond Moley said:

> We agreed that the heart of our difficulty was the anarchy of concentrated economic power which, like a cannon loose on a frigate's deck, tore from one side to another, crushing those in its path. But we felt that the remedy for this was not to substitute muskets for cannon or to throw the cannon overboard. We believed that any attempt to atomise big business must destroy America's greatest contribution to a higher standard of living for the body of the citizenry—the development of mass production. We agreed that equality of opportunity must be preserved. But we recognised that

> competition as such was not inherently virtuous. . . . So
> we turned from the nostalgic philosophy of the "trust
> busters" . . .

What Moley saw as government assistance for "a balanced and dynamic economic system" did not appear so to Hoover. The concept of the N.R.A. was, he said, a regimented "economy of scarcity . . . an idea that increased costs, restricted production and hampered enterprise will enrich a Nation". It encouraged monopoly and hit small businesses. In March 1934, F.D.R. appointed a board headed by Clarence Darrow, the Chicago criminal lawyer and liberal, to determine the validity of the charges. He found them substantially proved and found that the codes had fostered monopolistic practices. By 1935, the Administration was coming to agree that the N.R.A. was cumbersome and complicated. It may well be that it was relieved when the Court pronounced it unconstitutional.

If the measures to help the farmer did not meet the same degree of criticism—for it could be argued that the farmer's effort to bring his production into line with demand was no more than what industry did regularly, smoothly, and successfully—and if farmers became New Deal men—yet a philosophy of negation was hard to justify except as pure expediency. The two dramatic illustrations of production control—the slaughter of six million pigs and the destruction of cotton crops ready for picking—confirmed the image abroad of the United States as ruthless and selfish. "The more sincerely one believes that such legislation was an emergency necessity the more terrible is the indictment of the civilisation

which brought it about", thundered Norman Thomas.
And surpluses in any event recurred. The farmer's condition improved—but at fantastic cost.

Politically, this brought in dividends. If the Administration was losing the support of business by 1934,
it was gaining the support of the farmer, the worker, and
the Negro. It is rare for the party in power in the United
States to increase its congressional representation in a
non-presidential election year. But in 1934 the Democrats
won 332 seats in the House of Representatives against 313
in 1932, and their representation in the Senate rose from
50 to 69. The Democratic Party became more clearly the
party of the city and farm worker, of western agrarians and
of the Negro—and it was clear that for such groups, the
President, and not least his wife, had obvious sympathy.

But of practical success the verdict has to be less
sanguine. In the early part of 1933 unemployment
dropped sharply, but in January 1934 it rose again to
12,000,000 and in November, when the elections were
held, it was 11,000,000. Industrial production had fallen:
it was only one-third of the way towards the 1929
figures. Business morale was low. And agricultural prices
were far below the pre-1929 figures. The President, a
master of political moods, skilful at communicating his
own confidence by fire-side chats over the radio and by
regular press conferences—on both instruments he could
give virtuoso performances—was not master of the
economic situation.

It was his mastery of the political mood that led to the
"second" New Deal, where more genuine reforms were
enacted. To this Roosevelt was driven not only by

economic failure but by lessons he could read without benefit of economic punditry.

In Louisiana emerged the share-the-wealth movement of the "Kingfish", Huey Long, with his demand that the Government should guarantee an income of $5,000 a year to every family in the country, a country where, he believed, "Every man is a king, every woman a queen, but no one wears a crown." It is easy now to sneer at Long as a Messiah of the red-necks, with manners that were crude and an ambition that was rampant. When he came to lunch at Hyde Park, the President's mother, a dowager empress who did not need a crown, eyed him beadily, and asked her son in a penetrating whisper, "Who is that horrible man?" But Long's assassination— perhaps at the hands of his own bodyguard—removed one whom some men could see as a threat and some could see as a rival. Nor was Louisiana *sui generis*. Father Coughlin, the radio-priest of the Shrine of the Little Flower in Detroit, was calling for nationalisation of the banks and of the national resources and for more inflation. Upton Sinclair, whose volume of 1906 had done so much to stir Uncle Teddy to awareness of conditions in the meat-packing industry in Chicago, was now calling for a programme of End Poverty In California (E.P.I.C.) on which he almost won the Governorship of the State. And in the same happy state, where exotic plans flowered as thick as its own bougainvillaea, Dr Francis Townshend saw a simple solution for economic ills: give everyone who reached sixty and had a good character a government pension of $200 a month, on condition that they spend it before the next pay-day. Not surprisingly Dr Townshend

had many followers: there were in the end 3,000
Townshend clubs across the country. And from John L.
Lewis and the newly formed C.I.O. there came a more
serious demand for genuine support for the trade-union
movement.

The extent of the mid-term electoral victory of 1934,
and now this popular movement, undoubtedly im-
pressed the President, and there came a sharp shift in his
policy. "A decent living throughout life is an ambition
to be preferred to the appetite for great wealth and
great power." Moley saw it all as a shift from a theory of
Concentration and Control to one of Atomisation, and
left the government to those adherents of Brandeis, like
Corcoran, who preached the "curse of bigness". But the
legislative measures of the Second New Deal had been
long in the Congressional melting pot, and Congress
after 1934 had a will of its own. The scale of unemployment suggested that the theory of a directed rather than a
planned economy, of a happy consensus of Government,
industry, and labour was illusory. Berle, Moley, and
Tugwell were out; Hopkins was in. And so were
Frankfurter and the men brought up on Keynes. The
economy that was revived was mixed and capitalist, a
compensated, not a directed economy. And so there
came demands now for more daunting legislation. First,
a Works Progress Administration with a five-billion
dollar budget—the money to come from borrowing, not
taxes; despite the many splendid projects built under its
auspices, and the aid it provided for artists and writers,
it was seen as a form of political patronage. Hopkins, the
administrator, was charged with saying that "We shall

spend and spend and elect and elect"; true or otherwise, the W.P.A. led business men now to see F.D.R. as enemy No. 1. It was followed by the Social Security Act providing protection against old age and unemployment, on lines long familiar in Britain; by steeper inheritance taxes; and not least by the Wagner Act giving protection to the unions and their bargaining power—a measure that the President had earlier shelved and which he approved only in the most restrained terms. Much of this legislation had less obviously the hall-marks of F.D.R. personally. He had in no way encouraged the Wagner Act. But it brought him permanently a dividend he could appreciate, the support of labour. His re-election in 1936 was the greatest electoral triumph in American history; he won 46 of the then 48 states, all but Maine and Vermont; "as Maine goes, so goes Vermont". On a bridge leading from New Hampshire to Maine appeared the placard: "You are now leaving the United States". As he put it, everyone was against him—except the electorate.

And yet, in 1937, the economy was in decline once more. Industrial production slumped right through the year; and it slumped precisely as the Government stopped spending. The boom of 1933 and the boom of 1935–6 were caused, it seems, by Government spending and by that alone, and not by theories of direction, control, or of any mixture of the two. By 1937 there were bitter disputes in the steel and automobile industries. Unemployment, which had fallen below 5,000,000 in August 1937, rose to 9,600,000 in May 1938. The President lost political support even in his own party with his attack on the Supreme Court—perhaps the major political error of his career. And by 1937 he was losing his grip on Congress: he failed to persuade it to approve his plan for seven regional conservation authorities, to pass agricultural legislation, to approve his plan for minimum wages and maximum hours, or to carry his plan for administrative reorganisation. He failed particularly in 1938 when in the mid-term elections he sought to "purge" the members of Congress by supporting the re-election of some and opposing others. His numbers in the House—though still a majority—fell to 262. It was in fact the end of the New Deal. After 1938 the important questions became questions of foreign policy. On this subject F.D.R. had said hardly anything until 1937. Yet it was, paradoxically, his role here that was to give him a second chance to play the part of a liberal crusader; and it was after 1938 the war effort, or preparation for it, that solved the unemployment problem.

Roosevelt was not the author of the New Deal. It came partly from his lieutenants; it came partly out of the past; it came partly from Hoover. Many of the agricultural reforms had been discussed by the Coolidge administration; the content of the N.I.R.A. came largely from the Chambers of Commerce and the trade association movement of the Twenties; the T.V.A. was Norris's handiwork, the Wagner Act Wagner's. The second New Deal went through Congress with vast majorities and clearly represented a national demand. By 1937 the President had disrupted his party and ceased to control Congress. Nor did the New Deal end the Depression or large-scale unemployment. It left, however, some impressive achievements behind, however motivated: T.V.A., the Wagner Act, social security; and in restoring to many workers their own self-respect, the Roosevelt relief programme left his name a treasured memory in many of the areas blighted by the Depression, from New York to Oklahoma.

And the man in the White House? One verdict on him is that of James MacGregor Burns, who sees him as a superb leader without settled convictions, a manipulator perfectly adapted to the political climate, a tactician sanctified by his own skill at the profession of politics. The only appropriate verdict, he thinks, is Machiavelli's.

> A prince must imitate the fox and the lion, for the lion cannot protect himself from traps and the fox cannot defend himself from wolves. One must therefore be a fox to recognize traps and a lion to frighten wolves. Those that wish to be only lions do not understand this. Therefore, a prudent ruler ought not to keep faith when by so doing it would be against his interest and when the reasons which made him bind himself no longer exist. If men were all good, the precept would not be a good one; but as they are bad, and would not observe their faith with you, so you are not bound to keep faith with them.

Dr Schlesinger has a deeper insight into the personality and the inner loneliness of the man.

> The public face, all grin and gusto, had been carefully cultivated at Groton and Harvard; illness had made it second nature. But behind the cordiality and exuberance there remained an impassable reserve which many reconnoitered but none could penetrate. The relentless

buoyancy was less an impulse of the soul than a mark of cheer to the world, in part spontaneous enough, but more a defense against pity without and discouragement within. . . . Underneath there remained the other man— tougher than the public man, harder, more ambitious, more calculating, more petty, more puckish, more self- fish, more malicious, more profound, more complex, more interesting. . . . Detachment endowed him with a capacity for craftiness in politics and for calculation, sometimes even for cruelty, in human relations. Those who loved him best he teased most mercilessly. Nearly everybody was expendable.

SELECT BIBLIOGRAPHY

1. GENERAL

BROCK, W. R. *The Character of American History*. London (Macmillan) 1960.

FRANKLIN, J. H. *From Slavery to Freedom: a history of American Negroes*. New York (Knopf) 1956.

HAWGOOD, J. *The American West*. London (Eyre & Spottiswoode) 1967.

HIGHAM, J. *The Reconstruction of American History*. Torchbooks, New York (Harper) 1962.

HOFSTADTER, R. *The American Political Tradition and the men who made it*. London (Cape) 1962.

JONES, M. *American Immigration*. Chicago (University Press) 1960.

KENNEDY, J. F. *Profiles in Courage*. London (Hamish Hamilton) 1960.

PARKMAN, F. *The Oregon Trail*. New York (Modern Library) 1949.

SMITH, N. H. *Virgin Land*. New York (Vintage Paperback) 1957.

DE TOCQUEVILLE, A. *Democracy in America*. London (Oxford University Press) 1946.

WEBB, W. P. *The Great Plains*. New York (Grosset) 1957.

2. GEORGE WASHINGTON

Basic Writings of George Washington, ed. Saxe Commins. New York (Random House) 1948.

FREEMAN, D. S. *George Washington: a biography*, 7 vols. New York (Scribners) 1948–57. The most detailed and authoritative of the lives.

HUGHES, R. *George Washington*, 3 vols. New York (Morrow) 1926–30. The most readable life, but incomplete.

KNOLLENBERG, B. *Washington and the Revolution, a Re-appraisal*. London (Macmillan) 1940. The best and most challenging study of Washington as Commander-in-Chief.

STEPHENSON, N. W. and DUNN, W. H. *George Washington*. New York (Oxford University Press) 1940.

The Washington Papers, ed. Saul Padover. New York (Harper) 1955.

WEEMS, M. L. *The Life of Washington*, ed. M. Cunliffe. Cambridge (Harvard University Press) 1962.

WRIGHT, E. *Washington and the American Revolution*. London (English Universities Press) 1957.

The Writings of George Washington, 39 vols., ed. J. C. Fitzpatrick. Washington (Bicentennial Commission) 1931–44. A collection of 17,000 documents and letters prepared under direction of the United States George Washington Bicentennial Commission and published by authority of Congress.

3. BENJAMIN FRANKLIN

Benjamin Franklin, ed. H. W. Schneider. The American Heritage Series, New York (Liberal Arts Press) 1952. Contains Franklin's *Autobiography* and a good selection from his other writings.

BRIDENBAUGH, C. and J. *Rebels and Gentlemen, Philadelphia in the Age of Franklin*. London (Oxford University Press) paperback 1962.

Mr Franklin, a selection from his personal letters, eds. L. W. Labaree and W. J. Bell, Jr. New Haven (Cumberlege for Yale University Press) 1956. A publication from the project "The Papers of Benjamin Franklin" sponsored by Yale University Press.

The Papers of Benjamin Franklin, 10 vols. to date. Eds. L. W. Labaree *et al.* New Haven (Yale University Press) 1959– .

VAN DOREN, C. *Benjamin Franklin*. New York (Viking Press) 1956. The best of the biographies.

WRIGHT, E. *Benjamin Franklin and American Independence*. London (English Universities Press) 1966.

The Writings of Benjamin Franklin, 10 vols., ed. A. H. Smyth. New York (Macmillan) 1905–7.

4. ALEXANDER HAMILTON

ABERNETHY, T. P. *The Burr Conspiracy*. New York (Oxford University Press) 1954.

Alexander Hamilton and the Founding of the Nation, ed. R. B. Morris. New York (Dial) 1957.

DAUER, M. J. *The Adams Federalists*. Baltimore (Johns Hopkins University Press) 1953.

DORFMAN, J. *The Economic Mind in American Civilization*, 3 vols. New York (Viking Press) 1946–9.

HAMILTON, A., MADISON, J. and JAY, J., *The Federalist Papers*, ed. Rossiter. Mentor Books, London (Muller) 1961.

KURTZ, S. G. *The Presidency of John Adams.* University Park (University of Pennsylvania Press) 1957.

MITCHELL, B. *Alexander Hamilton,* 2 vols. New York (Macmillan) 1957, 1962.

SCHACHNER, N. *Alexander Hamilton.* New York (Appleton Century) London (Yoseloff) 1946.

5. ABRAHAM LINCOLN

CASH, W. J. *The Mind of the South.* New York (Knopf) 1960.

The Collected Works of Lincoln, 9 vols., ed. R. P. Basler. New Brunswick, N.J. (Rutgers University Press) 1953–5. Well edited and annotated.

CRAVEN, A. *The Coming of the Civil War.* Chicago (University Press) 1957. The War seen as a needless "repressible conflict".

The Lincoln Reader, ed. P. M. Angle. New Brunswick, N.J. (Rutgers University Press) 1947. A useful anthology.

The Living Lincoln, eds. P. M. Angle and E. S. Miers. New Brunswick, N.J. (Rutgers University Press) 1955. An excellent single-volume compilation.

NEVINS, A. *Ordeal of the Union,* 2 vols. New York (Scribners) 1947.
— *The Emergence of Lincoln,* 2 vols. New York (Scribners) 1950.

POTTER, D. M. *Lincoln and His Party in the Secession Crisis.* New Haven (Yale University Press) 1942. Excellent studies.

STAMPP, K. M. *And the War Came.* Baton Rouge (Louisiana State University) 1950. The author maintains that the War could not have been averted.
— *The Peculiar Institution.* London (Eyre & Spottiswoode) 1964. A good study of slavery as a social and economic system in the South.

THOMAS, B. P. *Abraham Lincoln.* London (Eyre & Spottiswoode) 1953. The best single-volume biography.

VANN WOODWARD, C. *Reunion and Reaction.* New York (Peter Smith) 1951.
— *The Strange Career of Jim Crow.* London (Oxford University Press) 1957.

6. WOODROW WILSON

BAILEY, T. A. *Woodrow Wilson and the Great Betrayal.* New York (Macmillan) 1945.
— *Woodrow Wilson and the Lost Peace.* New York (Macmillan) 1944.

BAKER, R. S. *Woodrow Wilson: Life and Letters*, 8 vols. New York (Scribners) 1927–39. The "official" biography, thoroughly documented.

BELL, H. C. F. *Woodrow Wilson and the People*. New York (Doubleday Doren) 1945. Excellent brief life.

BLUM, J. M. *Woodrow Wilson and the politics of morality*. London (A. & C. Black) 1956.

GEORGE, A. L. and J. L. *Woodrow Wilson and Colonel House: a personality study*. New York (John Day) 1956.

The Intimate Papers of Colonel House, 4 vols. ed. C. Seymour. London (Benn) 1926–8.

LINK, A. *Woodrow Wilson and the Progressive Era 1910–1917*. New York (Harpers) 1954.

— *Wilson, the Road to the White House*. Princeton (University Press) 1947.

— *Wilson, the New Freedom*. Princeton (University Press) 1956.

— *Wilson, the Diplomatist*. Princeton (University Press) 1957.

— *Wilson, confusions and crises*. Princeton (University Press) 1964.

— *Wilson, campaigns for Progressivism and Peace*. Princeton (University Press) 1966.

7. FRANKLIN D. ROOSEVELT

BURNS, J. M. *Roosevelt: The Lion and the Fox*. New York (Harcourt Brace) 1956. London (Secker & Warburg) 1957.

FREIDEL, F. *Franklin D. Roosevelt*. Boston (Little Brown) 1952.

GALBRAITH, J. K. *The Great Crash, 1929*. London (Hamish Hamilton) 1955.

HOOVER, H. C. *Memoirs*, 3 vols. New York (Macmillan) 1951–2.

ICKES, H. *Secret Diary*, 3 vols. New York (Simon & Schuster) 1953–4.

JOHNSON, W. *1600 Pennsylvania Avenue*. Boston (Little Brown) 1960.

MOLEY, R. *After Seven Years*. New York (Harpers) 1939.

PERKINS, D. *The New Age of Franklin Roosevelt 1932–45*. Chicago (University Press) 1957. An admirably balanced survey.

PERKINS, F. *The Roosevelt I Knew*. New York (Viking Press) 1946.

SCHLESINGER, A. M. *The Age of Roosevelt:* Vol. I, *The Crises of the Old Order 1919–33*; Vol. II, *The Coming of the New Deal*; Vol. III, *The Politics of Upheaval*, Boston (Houghton Mifflin) London (Heinemann) 1957–61.

TUGWELL, R. G. *The Democratic Roosevelt*. New York (Doubleday) 1957.

WECTER, D. *The Age of the Great Depression 1929–41*. New York (Macmillan) 1948.